FOOTBALL
for
COACHES *and* PLAYERS

GLENN SCOBEY WARNER

FOOTBALL
FOR COACHES & PLAYERS

A reprint of the 1927 Glenn S. "Pop" Warner classic

Carlisle, Pennsylvania

All new material copyright 2007 Tuxedo Press

Published by Tuxedo Press
Carlisle, PA 17015
LoneStarDietz.com

All rights reserved. No part of this publication may be reproduced, stored in a retrieval system, or transmitted, in any form or by any means, electronic, mechanical, photocopying, recording, or otherwise, without the prior permission of Tuxedo Press.

ISBN-10 0-9774486-4-9
ISBN-13 978-0-9774486-4-7
Library of Congress Control Number: 2007902236

DEDICATED to the hundreds of young men whom I have had the pleasure of coaching during the past thirty-three years, who by their courage, skill, and loyalty have enabled me to gain such success as I have had as a football coach.

PREFACE

In 1908 I published a correspondence course for football coaches and players. At that time the game was in the process of being revamped from the old push-and-pull, close-formation game into the more open game of today, in which forward passing has become an important factor in ground-gaining tactics. Radical changes had been made in the rules in 1906, notably that ten yards should be gained in four downs instead of five yards in three downs as was the rule up to that time. Pushing and pulling, and momentum involving more than one man, were prohibited, and the forward pass was legalized to strengthen the attacking power and to scatter the secondary defense. Since these changes were in the nature of experiments, and were revolutionary in character, naturally many rule changes had to be made for several succeeding years in order to regulate and adjust the new game to effect a proper balance between offense and defense. During those years of rather radical changes in the rules, no one had the courage to get out a book on the game, because rule changes would be likely to render such a book out of date after one season. Old methods and systems of play were being made obsolete, and football coaches were pretty much "up in the air." That state of affairs prompted me to publish a correspondence course, in pamphlet form, to aid the younger and less experienced coaches. That course was so well received, and I received so many letters of appreciation from those who availed themselves of its help, that I was encouraged to revise and publish the course in book form in 1912, by which time the rules had become fairly well settled. This book was about the first one of its nature to be published, and the edition has long since been sold out. Since then several coaches of established reputation have published books on football which have been very well received, and which have been of great help both to other coaches, especially the younger and more inexperienced men, and to players who have sought to further their knowledge of the game. These books supplied the demand in recent years, but the game is still developing, and the rules are still being changed somewhat from year to year; in fact, rather radical changes have been made during the present year. It would seem, therefore, that the time is ripe for a new textbook on the game, and with that thought in mind I have revised, rewritten, and enlarged my former book with the idea of making this work a complete text on football for the use of coaches and players.

Several coaches with whom I have talked regarding the publishing of this book have expressed the thought that I would probably not want to publish many inside facts, especially regarding the plays which I myself have been, and am still, using. And they will no doubt be rather surprised and perhaps incredulous when I state that this book outlines the exact methods I have been using myself, and contains plays all of which I have been using in recent years or am using now. There are no plays of an experimental character diagrammed in this book. All of them have been found in actual competition to be effective, and there is no play which I have found to be practical and effective which I have attempted to conceal from my readers.

I have not departed from the basic offensive formation which I have used for twenty years, except to change and perfect certain plays and perhaps add or discard a few plays each year. The plays diagrammed in this book are from that basic formation, or variations of it, as they have been developed up to this time. I expect in the future, as in the past, to be able to add to and vary these plays enough from year to year to keep coaches of rival teams guessing to some extent, and I have no fear of lessening my efficiency as a coach by giving to other coaches the methods, tactics, and plays which I have employed. Good football scouts get the information by watching my teams play; so I see nothing to gain by withholding from publication any pet plays or methods. There are no miracle coaches, and no coach has any great secrets or any unsolvable plays which make him successful. The successful coaches are those who know how to handle men, who pay great attention to a thorough teaching of the rudiments of the game, who have a comparatively few basic plays which they can teach their teams to execute faultlessly, and who have good material to work with.

I have used drawings to illustrate methods, rudiments, stances, and so forth, because I figure these are better than reproductions of photographs for this purpose. The better drawings have been made by William H. Deitz, who was a player and later my assistant while I was at the Carlisle Indian School, and who has since had a very successful coaching career. He is not only a very able football coach, but an artist as well, and I am greatly indebted to him for his help in illustrating this book. The simpler drawings and those not so well executed I have done myself.

I have read and studied with a great deal of interest all the books on the gridiron sport which have been published heretofore, and I have gained a great deal of knowledge from them. Every coach of any prominence must have ideas and information which are helpful to others in the same field of work. No one coach knows all about the game and the teaching of it, and there is a considerable difference of opinion regarding many phases of the game. I hope that the readers of this book may find ideas and suggestions which will prove helpful to them whether they be coaches or players.

GLENN SCOBEY WARNER

STANFORD UNIVERSITY
May 1927

CONTENTS

	PAGE
FOOTBALL, COACH AND PLAYER	1
EQUIPMENT	5
TRAINING, AND THE TREATMENT AND PROTECTION OF INJURIES	14
PRACTICE FIELD EQUIPMENT	23
THE RUDIMENTS	29
TACKLING	30
BLOCKING AND INTERFERENCE	36
FALLING ON THE BALL	42
PUNTING	45
JUDGING AND CATCHING PUNTS	48
PLACE-KICKING	52
DROP-KICKING	57
KICKING OFF	60
FORWARD PASSING	62
CATCHING FORWARD PASSES	68
THE LATERAL PASS	70
LINE PLAY	72
HOW TO PLAY END	78
HOW TO PLAY TACKLE	84
HOW TO PLAY GUARD	90
HOW TO PLAY CENTER	95
HOW TO PLAY THE BACKFIELD	100
FOOTBALL PRACTICE	110
SYSTEMS OF SIGNALS	118
SCOUTING	124
PSYCHOLOGY	127
OFFENSE	130
FORMATION A	136
FORMATION B	156
PUNT FORMATION	173
KICKING GOAL	186
RETURNING THE KICK-OFF	187
DEFENSE	188
GENERALSHIP	194

FOOTBALL, COACH AND PLAYER

Football has become the most important college and school sport. It is the sport in which students, alumni, and the general public take the greatest interest, and in fact this American college game has rapidly come to be the most popular of all amateur athletic contests. There are several reasons for this great and growing popularity. Football, unlike other games such as baseball, basketball, and so on, is a personal contact game, and there always has been and always will be a keen interest in this type of contest. The public likes to see a battle, if it is properly and fairly conducted. The game as played by the colleges and schools is free from all suspicion of crookedness, and there is always such keen rivalry between the teams playing that there is a snap and dash about the game which is usually absent from professional sports, especially professional football. It is a game requiring teamwork and strategy of the highest order, and the nature of the sport, requiring as it does a maximum of effort on the part of every player on both teams in nearly every play, makes it necessary that all the players be in perfect physical condition. For these reasons the spectators realize that, at a football game, they are witnessing a battle between twenty-two well-trained and well-nigh perfect physical specimens of young manhood who are struggling with a maximum of effort in a game which requires strength, speed, skill, endurance, and, most of all, such brains and strategy as are not required to so high a degree in any other sport.

The great and growing popularity of football has been of more value to college and school athletics than can ever be realized or estimated. The gate receipts from this sport have financed other branches of athletics which are just as important in developing the youth of our country, but which do not catch the public fancy to such an extent, and therefore have not been self-supporting financially. In many institutions in former years there was no provision made for outfitting teams and fostering athletics, and consequently there was a lack of interest and a scarcity of participants in sports. Students cannot be expected to take much interest in athletics if they are poorly equipped, have poor training quarters, gymnasiums, running tracks, and athletic fields, and have either incompetent coaches or perhaps none at all. Money had to be raised by subscription and by taxation of students, and the strictest economy had to be practiced. The income from football has largely remedied this deplorable situation, and the greatly increased interest and participation in other branches of athletics has been largely due to football.

Football requires and develops courage, co-operation, loyalty, obedience, and self-sacrifice. It develops quick thinking and cool-headedness under stress; it promotes clean living and habits; it creates self-confidence and the idea of service; it teaches control of temper; and most of all, it teaches that results worth while cannot be attained without perseverance, patience, and great effort. The player who does not have courage, who objects to hard work, who is not willing to deny himself many worldly pleasures during the playing season, and who is not willing to subject himself to strict discipline and to make sacrifices when necessary for the good of the team, is not a welcome member of any football squad, because the game requires all those qualities.

Wealth, poverty, social standing, race, and religion cut no figure on the football field. All coaches judge their players solely by their performance on the field of play. The one requirement should be that every candidate for the team be first of all a student, and not simply a football player who is likely to be dropped by the faculty at a critical time for failure in his studies.

It would be fatal for a coach to show favoritism, and he must be very careful to develop among his pupils a reputation for fairness and justice to all. He must have the confidence and respect of the players, and he should be very careful of his personal habits and conduct, both on and off the field, because he comes in such close contact with the players and the students that he wields a powerful influence. Faculty athletic committees, heads of institutions, and others whose business it may be to select athletic coaches, are becoming more and more careful that the men they choose for these positions are men of the very best character. That qualification is of first importance. The day of the roughneck, slave-driving, bulldozing coaches is over, and their methods are no longer tolerated in any well-regulated educational institution. Besides having a good character, a coach must be thoroughly equipped with a technical knowledge of the game in all its many phases, and he must be able to impart his knowledge to others. He must be a strict disciplinarian, and he should have a pleasing and likeable personality. He should be a good judge of the many different types of mental and physical characteristics among his pupils in order that he may handle them in such a way as to get the best results and may place them in the positions for which they are best fitted. With all these qualifications a coach must be energetic and enthusiastic, and he should be able to inspire his pupils in such a way that they will go about their practice and into their games with great interest and determination. A coach must be a master of details; he should overlook nothing that might be of the least help in developing his team and winning his games. A lost or worn-out cleat on a shoe might cause a player to slip and miss his tackle, thus enabling the opponents to score the winning touchdown.

A coach should be a good sportsman and should teach good sportsmanship to his pupils. Opponents should be treated with respect and the taking of unfair advantage should never be tolerated. A coach should play fair with rival coaches and teams and should always insist that his pupils play the game in a gentlemanly manner. He should allow no cursing and no dirty talk on the practice field, in the dressing room, nor in the games. The coach should be a good loser. He should congratulate the winners and give them full credit when his team is defeated, and he should refrain from excuses and alibis. Even though greatly disappointed in a game he should not vent his feelings upon his players by harsh and perhaps unjust criticism. The players on a losing team generally feel the sting of defeat as keenly as does the coach, and as a general rule the wise coach will try to revive the depressed spirit of his team rather than aggravate it by harsh criticism. If after a defeat he is in no mood to do this, he should at least wait until the team comes out for practice on Monday before saying anything. By that time the coach will have had plenty of time to think things over and to analyze the causes of defeat, and thus he may be able to offer constructive criticism instead of heaping abuse, perhaps undeserved, upon his charges. I have seen some coaches who became so exasperated over unexpected defeats, probably caused by their own failure to curb overconfidence and to impart the proper mental attitude toward their opponents, that they ordered their players out early Monday afternoon and scrimmaged and drove them so brutally throughout the week that their vitality was sapped and their spirit broken to such an extent that they made a failure of what should have been, with proper handling on the part of the coach, a successful season.

My experience has taught me that a coach should at all times be patient, be sympathetic, be firm, and be fair. He should never lose his temper nor become exasperated by the mistakes of his players.

EQUIPMENT

The equipment of the players is a very important consideration, and there has been a steady improvement made in the wearing apparel and protectors of football players. In the early days of the game, heavy moleskin trousers, heavy worsted jerseys, heavy wool stockings, and rather cumbersome shoes were the thing. Jerseys and trousers were heavily padded with soft cotton or hair pads on shoulders, elbows, hips, thighs, and knees. Canvas jackets were common and nose guards and shin guards were very much in vogue. Durability was about the first requisite because athletic managements were generally short of funds. Head gears were not invented in the early days and for head protection players let their hair grow long—so long in fact that I have seen many a tackle by the hair.

The tendency since the early days of the game has been to lighten the wearing apparel, to dispense with padding and protectors which could safely be done away with, and to protect more adequately the shoulders and thighs, which are the places of most frequent contact between the players, the shoulders doing the charging and tackling and the thighs receiving the impact of opponents' shoulders and heads when being tackled or blocked.

The wave of development toward lighter equipment, like all waves of various kinds, has really swept beyond what will eventually be found a normal and sensible balance between extreme lightness affording very little protection, and unnecessarily heavy and cumbersome clothing. Silk and satin trousers have been used and found lacking in durability, and some teams have gone so far as to use short padless and kneeless trousers such as are worn by basketball, soccer, and rugby players. In my opinion that is carrying the idea of lightness to an extreme. Light canvas or khaki is both light in weight and durable, and silk or kneeless trousers are simply fads which will soon be relegated to the past.

While lightness in equipment is essential, durability is an important consideration because the game is a rough one, destructive of players' wearing apparel, and replacements of clothing are rather expensive. It pays to use good equipment. There is no economy in buying cheap and flimsy goods which will soon wear out, and which even when new probably will not adequately serve the purposes for which they are worn. At the same time it is not necessary to procure the most expensive clothing and protectors. All sporting goods dealers provide ultra-expensive trousers, headgears, shoulder pads, shoes, and so forth, for those universities which seek the very best and most expensive equipment. These high-priced articles are generally made of needlessly expensive materials and are of unnecessarily elaborate workmanship. As a general rule, just as good and serviceable clothing and protectors can be purchased for a reasonable price.

Where it can be afforded it is quite an advantage to equip the players, at least the twenty to thirty who are likely to be used in the games, with three sets of trousers and shoes: one set for practice during the week, in which durability and adequate protection are the main features, another set for the games on dry, firm fields, in which lightness and only absolutely necessary protection are the main points to consider, and the third set for use in games played on wet and soft fields where padding is unnecessary and light and waterproof material for trousers is advisable and longer cleats on the shoes are indispensable. The trousers and shoes used only in the games can be preserved generally for several seasons, so that the first expense, while rather heavy, need only be added to from year to year for replacements. It is a good plan to have shoes and trousers marked with the wearer's name and turned in after each game, to be kept in repair and in safety until the next.

The players should be taught economy in the care of their uniforms. Replacements should be made only when necessary, and all equipment should be kept in repair and at the end of the season gathered in for use by class and scrub teams the following season. It has been my experience that at some places there is much needless extravagance in the matter of equipment. Players get away with jerseys, shoes, and other articles, feeling that all they have to do is to ask the management for new ones. At many institutions with ample funds no protest is made against this petty thievery. Again, players will discard items of their uniforms for very little reason, merely in order to get new ones. These practices should be discouraged because they teach extravagance and cause a needless expense, and the amount of money spent on athletic teams has come to be a subject of some criticism. While the money for this needless extravagance may be ample at institutions where huge gate receipts are the rule, that is no adequate reason for squandering it needlessly. Funds for such expenditures could better be conserved and used for more useful and unquestionable purposes.

Shoes

The most important part of the player's outfit is his shoes, since without good footing a player is greatly handicapped in almost everything he attempts to do; not only that, but cheap or ill-fitting shoes are likely to cause sprained ankles and sore feet. The shoes should be strong but not too heavy, and they should be as broad across the ball of the foot and toes as the foot will stand, in order to provide plenty of room for the cleats and greater surface contact with the ground, resulting in a better foothold. This makes the shoes easier on the feet and decreases the liability of spraining the ankle by turning the foot sideways. Therefore by all means wear broad-toed shoes.

Unless strong leather ankle supporters are worn, the tops of the shoes should come well above the ankle so as to strengthen and support the ankle joints. Many players prefer to wear low shoes over leather ankle supporters as this allows a little more freedom to the ankle joints; but a rather high shoe, tightly laced, often renders an ankle supporter unnecessary. The ankle joint gives football players more trouble than any other part of the body, and nearly all ankle sprains are caused by a side turn of the foot. Broad-soled shoes will save some ankles, leather ankle supporters will prevent a great many more sprains, and high shoes are an added protection; but experience has proved to my satisfaction that the steel ankle brace, sewed into the shoe, almost wholly prevents side sprains of the ankle. Where these are in, and the shoes kept tightly laced, there need be no other ankle supporter worn, and the freedom of movement of the foot and ankle is not interfered with seriously.

The sole of the shoe should be just thick enough to provide a solid base for the cleats, which should be, for ordinary use, at least a half-inch long and so distributed over the sole of the shoe as not to hurt the foot by pressing through the sole. Care should be taken to have the cleats extend as near flush with the edges of the sole as possible, to prevent turning the foot over. There should be two or three small cleats on the heel, or one wide one extending clear across. The cleats for ordinary wear should be about three thicknesses of ordinary sole leather, nailed on with a row of nails driven in as close together as possible, the nails long enough so that they will clinch on the inside of the shoe. Cleats should be trimmed down with a knife as close to the heads of the nails as the rules permit, and should not be too broad at the base.

For dry fields and for ordinary use, the cleats should not be too long, not over five-eighths of an inch. They should be rather closely distributed over the sole of the shoe, and they should be as sharp as the rules allow so that they will sink into the hard field and not hold the player up off the ground. Cleats that are too long give the impression of the player being on stilts, and there is danger of injury to the ankles.

For wet or muddy fields, the cleats should be fewer and much longer. Too many extra-long cleats will simply clog up with dirt and mud and prove to be a handicap rather than a help. I have known many games to be lost because the winning team was properly shod whereas the losers could not secure good footing because of cleats unsuited to weather and field conditions.

Several firms are putting out shoes with detachable cone cleats which can be unscrewed and replaced with long mud-cleats when the occasion arises. There was some objection to these when they were first tried out because of the cleats breaking off or coming unscrewed, but this type of shoe has been greatly improved and is now quite practical.

Cone-shaped cleats, of rubber composition, fiber, or leather, are coming to be more popular than the rectangular style standard heretofore, but there is no great advantage in cone cleats. Fiber cleats can be secured in nearly all styles and heights with holes already drilled, and these fiber cleats are rapidly supplanting the sole-leather variety.

Rather high-top shoes should be worn in practice and in the less important games, and under these it is advisable to wear ankle supporters. The figure-eight type of canvas bandage is the most commonly used, but leather and elastic supporters are also

EQUIPMENT

good. Coaches and trainers should caution players to keep their shoes tightly laced, since this will insure better ankle protection.

In important games many players are permitted to wear very light and low-cut shoes. Protection is sacrificed here for speed. The ends and the backfield players need such shoes more than the five center men. Care should be taken that the players who do the kicking should wear shoes which are suitable for that work and with which they have been getting good results in practice. I have seen a good kicker's punts ruined in a game because he put on new light shoes with which he had had no punting practice. The same is true in goal kicking.

Stockings

Stockings are not a very important item of a player's outfit. In many localities where the weather is warm, and on any wet, muddy field, stockings are not worn at all. Instead short socks which come just above the shoe tops are used. Many teams wear cotton stockings because they are lighter and more durable than wool. Heavy stockings are not needed and only handicap the player by unnecessary weight, especially when they become soaked with mud, water, or perspiration.

Trousers

Next to the shoes the trousers are the most important part of the player's uniform. They should be made of canvas or khaki. Canvas is the cheaper and more durable material and is most generally used.

The trousers should be rather close fitting with as little surplus material in them as is compatible with comfort and freedom of movement. Trousers that are too tight are a severe handicap, while loose and baggy trousers are also to be avoided.

In the early days football trousers did not afford any kidney or short rib protection and there were rather frequent injuries to these parts. Of late years trousers are so made that they extend well above the belt, with padded fiber strips to cover and protect the lower back and sides. These are especially desirable because they afford necessary protection to those parts of the body so much used in clipping and blocking.

In practice and in the early and less important games knee pads should be worn. These can be of any soft material such as cotton, felt, hair, or sponge rubber; but foam rubber pads are best because this material is extremely light and does not absorb moisture as the other materials mentioned do. Where one set of trousers has to do both for practice and games, the knee pads should be detachable so that they can be removed when not needed; or they should be separate from the trousers and attached directly to the knee. These latter pads are really preferable because they are always in place and do not shift about as knee pads in the trousers often do.

Knee, hip, and other pads do not prevent sprained or wrenched joints but only help to prevent bruises. Consequently they are not very important or necessary except to be worn in practice to protect those parts of the body which are continually coming in contact with the ground or with the opposing players, and which would gradually, by repeated contact, become sore and tender. Therefore it is wise to wear such pads during practice and in early and less important games in order to protect every part of the body as much as possible. Late in the season when the fields are usually soft and the player is toughened by weeks of practice, he can easily do without soft padding for the important games without taking much chance of any serious injury. Certainly no soft pads should be used in playing upon a wet field, when they are not needed for protection and they handicap the players by taking up moisture and so adding useless weight.

The part of the body covered by the trousers which is the most liable to injury, and which is the hardest to protect, is the large muscle of the thigh. This is especially true of the backfield men or other players who carry the ball, since the thigh is the part which generally must bear the impact of collision with opponents who tackle them. It is therefore quite necessary that the thighs should be protected both in practice and in games, whether played on dry fields or not. Soft pads for this purpose, or quilted thighs in the trousers, are of no value and are little used. The cane and fiber strips so generally used afford some protection and are better than nothing, but what is needed is a hard, stiff, one-piece protector conforming to the shape of the leg and covering the front and side of the thigh. These should be fastened in the legs of the trousers or may be attached directly to the leg by means of adhesive tape. Such protectors will so distribute a hard blow over such a large surface that it can do no damage, whereas soft padding or protectors made of several pieces do not offer adequate resistance to impacts of the shoulders, heads, and knees of opponents.

When a game is played on a rainy day or upon a wet, muddy field it is well to change water-soaked, dirty trousers for light and dry ones during the intermission.

Jerseys

Lightness together with durability should be the distinguishing feature of football jerseys. Heavy jerseys are not desirable except in very cold weather. Cotton or cotton and wool mixture, or medium- or lightweight wool are the best materials. Elbow pads are not much used but are advisable in practice and when playing games on gravelly or hard and frozen fields. On soft fields they can easily be dispensed with. Such pads can be attached to the jersey sleeves, or better still they can be attached directly to the elbows and worn under the jersey.

It is quite comon to use some kind of material supposed to be less slippery than the jersey and sewed on to the sleeves and on the chest and under the arms of the garment as an aid to hanging on to the ball and to prevent fumbling. This "stickum" cloth does seem to have rather desirable qualities when it is first put on. But dirt and dust soon glaze it over and nullify its usefulness, and it is very doubtful if it has any merit, or enough to warrant the expense of attaching it. Powdered rosin dusted on the places where the ball is held, after first applying Karo corn syrup with a stiff brush, will give much better results. Ordinary shoe polish or floor wax on the hands will give a tacky and non-slippery grip that aids materially in preventing fumbles and is a great aid in forward passing.

Shoulder Pads

Shoulder pads are very important. It is with the shoulders that the players tackle, charge, and block, and these parts of the body have to withstand many shocks of collision between players. It is important that the shoulder pads give ample protection and at the same time are light in weight, afford perfect freedom of movement of the arms, and are comfortable. Soft padding is almost useless. What is needed is a protector of hard, unyielding material with a layer of soft padding on the side next to the shoulder and a convex hard surface on the outside. The pad should extend well down in front to protect the collar bone and should extend well over the point of the shoulder. There has been great improvement made by the sporting goods manufacturers in these protectors and there are many models which are very satisfactory. They need not be expensive. Some of the cheaper ones give just as good protection as the more elaborate and costly kind.

Head Gears

All players should wear head protectors or helmets during the games and scrimmage practice. These should be as light in weight as is compatible with adequate protection. They should come well down in front to just above the eyebrows, so as to prevent cuts over the eyes through the collisions which will occur often, and they should come well down in the back to protect the base of the brain. A bridged-over top, the helmet resting on webbing or leather supports rather than directly on the head, is much preferable to soft padding, since this method better distributes shocks. The ear protectors should have large holes in them to enable the wearer to hear plainly. In the ordinary helmet the ear holes are too small to insure good hearing. The holes are made small so that the ears cannot come through. Some sporting goods houses, at my suggestion, are now making the holes in the ear protectors much larger and covering them with fine wire gauze to prevent the ears from coming through the hole. It will be readily recognized that this is a very important matter when it is realized how much noise there is at a football game and how necessary it is that the players hear the signal and make no mistake in it. I have seen many games lost because when a team got near the opponent's goal where the tumult of cheering is always loudest some player misunderstood the signal and gummed up the play. Head helmets also should have plenty of ventilating holes in the crown.

Nose Guards, Shin Guards, and Supporters

Nose guards, rather commonly used in the early days of football, are no longer worn except by players suffering from broken or bruised noses.

EQUIPMENT

Shin guards have come to be very little worn in recent years and are only used temporarily to protect sore shins while they are recovering from bruises.

Supporters or jock-straps should be worn by all players at all times during the practice and in the games, and these should be changed or washed and disinfected frequently.

Underclothing

It is advisable for the players, especially during practice, to wear lightweight white cotton undershirts and stockings under their regular equipment. These should be washed frequently so that they will provide a clean and sanitary covering next to the skin and prevent skin poisoning from dyes in the regular jerseys and stockings. Moreover, they are less irritating than the outer woolen garments.

Heavy underclothing to keep the body warm in extremely cold weather is very important. Players cannot do their best when they are chilled by the very cold winds and weather occasionally encountered late in the season, and I have known of games being won by teams which were inferior to their opponents under ordinary conditions, but whose coaches were thoughtful enough to provide heavy underclothing which enabled the players to play in comfort, while their opponents were lightly clad and handicapped by being uncomfortably cold and chilled all through the games.

TRAINING, AND THE TREATMENT AND PROTECTION OF INJURIES

Before practice starts every candidate for the team should have a thorough physical examination by a competent physician in order to determine his fitness to engage in the strenuous exercise which the game of football demands. This examination should especially concern the candidate's heart and lungs. Great emphasis was properly placed upon physical fitness as the first requirement of our soldiers during the World War, and it was surprising how many young men were found to have weaknesses which unfitted them for the arduous duties of soldiering. Football playing and training demands just as good physical fitness for the work as do military duties, and no young man should be allowed to try for the team unless he is in a normally fit condition.

Coaches or trainers in charge should at the start of the training season give the players to understand just what is expected of them in the way of habits, diet, sleep, care of the body, and conduct on and off the field; and no player should report for practice unless he is willing to obey these rules and instructions and to make the little sacrifices that he has to make by giving up certain pleasures and habits—sacrifices that are advisable if he is to be in the best possible condition. The player who thinks he can slyly break the training rules, smoke an occasional cigarette, or keep late hours is all wrong and has no business to be trying for the team. He is almost sure to be found out sooner or later, and he is not only violating the trust placed in him, but he is doing himself and the team and coach a great injustice. A coach who tolerates such breaches of training on the part of any of his players is making a great mistake, because the players will soon come to the conclusion that they can violate the training rules without punishment. When they see one player—perhaps a star whom the coach dislikes to lose and so allows to remain on the squad—breaking training and getting away with it, they figure that they might as well do the same, and the team morale is thus destroyed, the reputation of the coach for discipline is ruined, and the players' respect for him is lessened. Any team or coach is much better off without the services of a star player who thinks he is so good that he can do as he pleases without danger of dismissal. The toleration of such a player will do more harm than good to the team, no matter how excellent a player he may be.

Rules of training for football players are about the same as for any branch of athletics in which endurance, strength, and quickness are required.

The use of tobacco or stimulants of any kind should be prohibited. At least eight hours of sleep should be required and regular hours for meals and for retiring should be insisted upon. Nothing should be eaten between meals and trips to the soda fountain should be discouraged.

The players should be cautioned against rough-housing off the field, and since they are in a way heroes among their associates, their conduct and influence should be such as to furnish a good example to the rest of the students.

Training tables are very advantageous when they can be afforded, because in addition to providing the right kind of food they provide a place off the field where the players congregate three times a day and get better acquainted and chummy. There they can talk over in periods of relaxation the happenings on the field, and may discuss the strong and weak features of the players and teams they are to meet on the field of play.

It is for this fostering of a friendly and brotherly team spirit that I regard the training table of the most value. However, it is not by any means necessary and can be dispensed with without any great handicap. Most football players have sense enough to know what food agrees with them and what does not, and I have never found that it was essential to insist upon a strict diet. A great many teams are provided with one meal each day at the training table. If this is feasible the meal should be in the evening. If one training-table meal cannot be afforded or is not practical, I have found that getting the team together for one meal a week, say on Tuesday or Wednesday evening, with a blackboard talk after dinner, serves the purpose very well.

The dressing and training rooms should be of ample size and should be well ventilated and heated. Great care should be taken that these rooms are kept clean; they should be disinfected at least once a week to prevent contagions of boils or skin diseases which are likely to be contracted during the season. A drying room for uniforms should be provided so that these can be dried between practices. No player likes to put on damp, cold, heavy clothing to go out for practice.

Players should be discouraged from spending too much time under hot showers because these have a weakening tendency. All skin eruptions, cuts, etc., should have an application of iodine or other suitable germicide after each practice.

When the football season starts the players who are to try for the team present themselves in every kind of physical condition. Some may have been working at manual labor, and so start training in good physical condition; others may have loafed all summer and start practice overweight and soft; still others may have overdone during the hot season and as a consequence find themselves underweight and run-down. All are anxious to make the team, and all start practice with a great deal of enthusiasm and determination.

It is a mistake very often made, even where there are supposed to be good trainers in charge, to start the training season with hard, rough work, giving the players no chance to work into it gradually. It is generally in the first two weeks of practice, when the players are full of ambition and determination, that they are most likely to overdo or get laid up with injuries which may keep them out of the game for the whole season. In my opinion the work for all the candidates should be about the same at this time. The soft, fat candidate will find light work hard for him and he will sweat and lose weight, but he will gradually become able to do hard work. The thin, overworked man needs the same light work to give him enough exercise to create a good appetite and make him sleep well; while the man who is already in good physical condition does not need more than the light practice the others are given. This work will be easy for him, and he will store up energy for use later in the season.

It would be unwise to work the soft, fat man hard at the start with the idea of taking off weight and hardening him up. More likely he will strain himself or get disgusted with the game and quit. It would be a mistake to be too easy on the player who is under weight, as he needs a moderate amount of work. Therefore I am of the opinion that all sorts of candidates will thrive, and keep in condition or gradually train up or down according to their needs, on the same moderate amount of work, gradually increased from week to week, until all are in good condition. Then care should be taken that they do not overdo and begin to lose their speed and aggressiveness.

When a player begins to lose interest in his work, when the practice becomes irksome and he hates to go to the field, it is time he took a day or two off before it is too late. He will find that with a short rest he will feel like getting into the game again, and he should be careful not to work too hard from that time on. The coach dislikes to have a player miss a day's practice and often makes the mistake of insisting upon daily attendance in cases when by laying a man off for a day or two days, or a week, he would save a good man for usefulness to the team. On the other hand, by working him when he shows signs of staleness the player is likely to be rendered useless for the balance of the season.

The same mistake is often made in handling a player who has suffered an injury. Too often his anxiety to get back into the game, together with the coach's fear that he will miss too much practice, causes him to start rough work too soon. The injury is made worse, and he is laid up for a long time, whereas by the use of a little patience and caution he would remain out of practice long enough to recover completely from the injury, and suffer no ill effects from it when starting rough work again.

Players will often deceive their coaches or trainers and will not mention an injury, or the fact that they are not feeling well, for fear that they will be laid off for a day or two and other players will get their places. The coach, not knowing that anything is wrong, will often misjudge a player who is unable to do his best work by reason of the injury. It would be much better for the player and for everyone else concerned if he would report all injuries or any indisposition to the coach or trainer, so that he might be treated at once. Thus the player so handicapped may not be sized up wrongly by those in charge.

So anxious are some players to get into a game that they will practice deception in this way and go into the game in no condition to play. In such cases their playing is likely to be so inferior as to queer them for the rest of the season. This sort of deception is not fair to the coaches, the rest of the team, nor to the player himself.

Under the heading "Equipment," it was explained how to protect the parts most liable to injury so as to avoid hurts as far as possible; but in spite of all precautions accidents are likely to happen. Injuries which are serious enough to keep a player from practice should be intelligently treated and patiently borne until recovery. As previously explained, the player should not be in too much of a hurry to jump into the game again.

Nature will cure all bruises and sprains, but it requires time for its healing. In the case of bruises, Nature can be aided by the proper use of electricity, heat, vibrating machines, and massage; but these, used to excess, will retard the recovery, and therefore they should only be employed by physicians or those who understand their use. Electricity and massage will also aid Nature in curing sprains, while good liniment applied in connection with massages will add to their effectiveness.

If the bruise is not a bad one, but simply painful to a blow, as for instance a bruised thigh muscle or "charley horse," a protector can be made which will prevent any hard blow from reaching the spot, and the player can continue his practice. Such a protector should be in the nature of a bridge, made from a piece of aluminum or fiber large enough to more than cover the tender spot, shaped to the part to be covered, and with its edges resting upon a strip of half-inch felt, so that all the pressure or concussion from any hard blow will be distributed through the felt all around the sore spot but not on it. This protector should be held in place by strips of adhesive plaster. With a protector of this kind properly made and adjusted, a "charley horse" or muscle bruise need not keep any player out of the game or practice. Such protectors are very useful in shielding boils and other painful spots, and are on the same principle as most cornpads, with the added protection of a cover or bridge which prevents anything from touching the injured part.

Adhesive tape comes in very handy and is much used by most teams for holding pads and protectors in place and for wrapping, bracing, and strengthening sprained or weak joints. Sprained ankles, probably the most troublesome and frequent of all football injuries, should be well taped with adhesive, care being taken to provide the greatest support and protection to the ligaments which are torn or strained. Sprained ankles properly taped will very quickly recover and only in severe cases need the injured players be forced to stay out of practice. Heat applications and gentle massage are very helpful. Only in the most severe cases, where the ligaments are badly torn, is it advisable that sprained ankles or other joints be encased in plaster casts. These latter prevent the light exercise of the injured joints which is advisable while the healing process is going on, and they also prevent massage and treatment. They are so weakening, since they prevent all exercise of the joint, that after recovery it takes considerable time to strengthen the joint enough for hard work to be done with it.

Broken or cracked ribs or torn cartilages between the ribs, and also sore hip bones, should be protected by plates of fiber or aluminum conformed to the body, padded around the edges with rather thick felt, and fastened over the injury and held in place by adhesive tape.

Sprained knees and floating cartilages in the knees are rather difficult to protect, but strips of adhesive tape which do not interfere with normal knee action are of service, and the joint should be strengthened and supported by elastic bandages or supporters. Hinged metal braces which prevent side movements and twisting are also very useful to protect weak or injured knee joints. These latter, in addition to their regular fastenings, should be taped on with adhesive tape to hold them in place and prevent slipping down.

The shoulders have to stand many hard knocks and unless they are properly protected they are likely to be injured. A rather frequent injury is the tearing of the ligaments which hold the collar bone in place at the point of the shoulder. This injury results in a small spot becoming very tender to the touch, and without protection a player having such an injury would be unable to use his shoulder without great pain. Such a hurt should first be tightly strapped with adhesive tape, the tape coming well down on the chest and back and pulled tightly over the injured part in order to hold the bone in place and strengthen the injured ligaments; then by the same method, and in the same manner as explained previously, a protector can be made in the nature of a bridge, resting on felt placed around the injured part, and the whole fitted and held in place by means of adhesive plaster. The ordinary pad should be placed over this, and the shoulder can be used and the injury will heal at the same time.

Pre-Season Training

I do not believe that it is advisable for football players to engage in hard manual labor during the summer. Hard physical labor over a part of the summer might benefit those who did practically no training during the school year after the close of the football season, but even then a period of comparative rest and relaxation should be taken a couple of weeks prior to the beginning of practice so as to recover the reserve strength and pep necessary at the start of the season. Players who have been in training a good share of the school year should rest and relax during the summer. No young man should be in training or be doing hard work throughout the year. If hard work has to be done, it would be best not to work in a hot locality, because excessive heat coupled with hard work will so sap the energy of any man that he will not have the necessary vitality, speed, and reserve strength that football playing requires. Many boys have the mistaken idea that they should do hard work requiring severe muscular exertion during the summer vacation so that they will come back for the football season as hard as nails. That is all wrong, and I have known many good athletes to come back to school in the fall under weight and so lacking in energy and enthusiasm that they did not get into good playing condition until long after the middle of the season. Exercise should be taken during the vacation of course, and there should be no dissipating; but light work and recreational sports are preferable to hard labor. If the player does not have a job, such games as tennis, handball, baseball, and others requiring speed and nimbleness furnish the best kind of exercise. Lying around on the beaches and swimming every day certainly will not do an athlete any great good.

Getting the players back a couple of weeks before school opens is a very good plan as a great deal can be accomplished in that period, when there is no study or other school duties required of the men. Morning and afternoon practices can be held during that time and much can be done to put the team in sufficiently good physical condition, to work up a semblance of team work, and to get the candidates fitted into their proper places before the first game of the season, which usually comes very soon after school or college opens.

Spring Practice

The football season is so short and the games come along so soon after the teams start training that it is advisable wherever practicable to have spring practice. Football, as no other game to so high a degree, requires team play. The plays have to be numerous enough to give diversity to the attack, and every man must learn both the play signals and the separate duties required of him in all those plays. To learn those plays and to enable each player to know instantly upon hearing the signal just what his part in each play is, is a matter requiring a great deal of practice and rehearsing of plays and signals. The coach should have his offense, especially the basic plays in it, all planned in advance, and he has to start at once to drill the team and substitutes in those plays. He has no time to experiment, to try out the new plays he may have figured out since the preceding season. It is a great advantage then if he has an opportunity to try out those new plays in practice before the regular season opens. He may find that most of his new conceptions are either worthless or no better than the plays he has already found to be useful, but in my own experience I have found by experiment each year that I have had spring practice a few good plays or variations of old ones which have been very useful when the regular season rolled around. This spring or off-season practice is of great value for that kind of laboratory work alone, and in addition it gives the players that much more practice and experience, and enables the coach to get a much better line on the different candidates for the team. At every institution it will be found that many of the good football men are busy training for the various spring sports, but there are also many who are not candidates for those sports, and these men should be prevailed upon to turn out. The game is becoming more and more scientific each year. More time is needed to work up the plays requiring great skill in handling the ball, such as double and triple passing, forward passing, etc., and spring practice is being resorted to more and more. In the South, where the weather permits, practice during the winter months is held and has proved a big advantage.

During these off seasons of practice the coach has time for many things which the short regular season does not permit. Besides experimenting with new plays he has time to try out the players in different positions to learn where they are likely to do the best work, and he can devote more time to rudimentary practice than is possible in the fall. He also can give his attention to the new and less experienced players who are most in need of coaching but who have to be neglected somewhat in the fall because of the rush to get the better and more experienced players welded into a workable machine. Very often it is found that the inexperienced player, if given coaching and encouragement, will eventually develop into a star.

PRACTICE FIELD EQUIPMENT

There are quite a number of devices which can be used on the practice field to facilitate the development of a football squad. A tackling dummy is almost indispensable for practicing tackling and blocking. Practicing these important rudiments on each other is too rough on the players for them to indulge in it to the extent that is necessary if they are to attain proficiency. Some practice in tackling and blocking each other should be required in addition to the practice afforded in actual scrimmage, but the dummy should be used for the bulk of this work. On another page several types of dummies are shown. A strong sack filled with sawdust and suspended from a tree limb, or from built-up supports, makes a very good substitute for a dummy. The dummy should be well away from the tree so that there will be no danger of injury to players, and if the dummy is suspended from a cross beam the posts supporting this beam should be far enough apart so that there is no danger of tacklers and blockers striking them. A dummy which will allow itself to be carried back and down and which will automatically come back into position again when released is the best arrangement. Several such types are shown in the drawings, one of which shows a dummy which can be pulled back and forth on a supporting rope so as to afford practice in tackling and blocking a moving object. The latest dummy which I have used with very satisfactory results is the last one shown, which is not only automatic in adjusting itself after each tackle, but which forces the tackler and blocker to hit the dummy low because the padded ring circling the dummy at the waist acts in the same way as the stiff arm of an opponent who is trying to ward off the tackler or blocker. This ring also makes it somewhat more difficult for the tackler to force the dummy to the ground and therefore gives a better imitation of the resistance which a real player would offer. The ring and the weight from which it is suspended are heavier than the dummy, so that when the dummy is hit and carried back and down the ring is pulled up, and when the dummy is released the weight and ring pull it back into place all ready for the next tackler.

Standing dummies which can be carried to different parts of

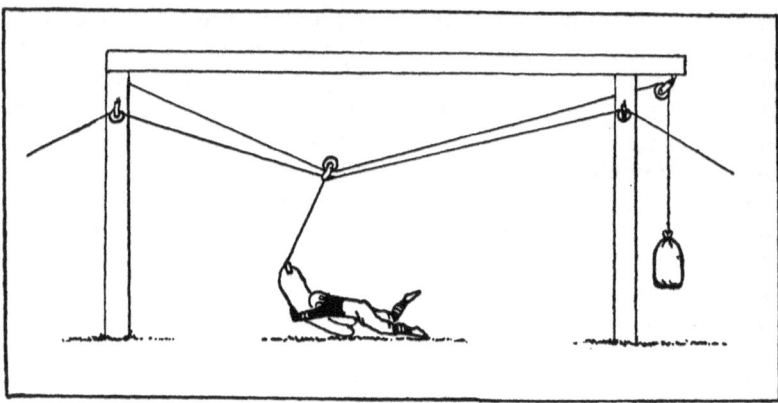

TACKLING DUMMIES

the field and used as defensive ends in signal practice or dummy scrimmage are very useful.

For practice in using the stiff-arm, in swinging the legs away from tacklers, and in developing pivoting, three or four posts set in the ground about ten yards apart and about three and one-half feet high come in very handy. These should be well padded on the top, to look something like large mushroom buttons. They can be placed in line at one side of the practice field, and the backs can get much valuable practice by zigzagging through them, using the posts as imaginary tacklers.

A charging sled is a very important asset for developing charging both with the shoulders and with stiff arms, and every practice field should by all means have one. These machines or sleds not only develop quickness in charging but afford much needed development of the leg drive and of the muscles of the back, and they are great conditioners for the linemen. Charging sleds with a padded board the whole length are not so good, because in charging with the shoulders the players' heads have to go over the padded boards and therefore the players have to turn their bodies instead of hitting squarely. Individual charging pads are much to be preferred because these allow the players' heads to go by the object, and they can charge squarely with their shoulders. The best device for this work is shown and described briefly on another page. This sled is so built that there is some give or spring to the blocking surfaces, and is a much better arrangement than the ordinary rigid type of pads since it enables the players to hit harder without danger of injuring themselves. The sled should be heavy enough so that there is considerable resistance to the charging players and it should not be placed on rollers to make it easy to push around. Any carpenter, by looking at the drawing and reading the description, can easily make one of these sleds. If it is well made it will last for several years, especially if it is set up off the ground on blocks during the seasons of the year when it is not being used.

Another device which I have used during the past two years and have found very helpful in developing the offense and rehearsing the plays is shown on another page. It is a dummy defensive team and really affords better practice than dummy scrimmage against another non-resisting team. Furthermore it releases such a team so that all the players can practice the

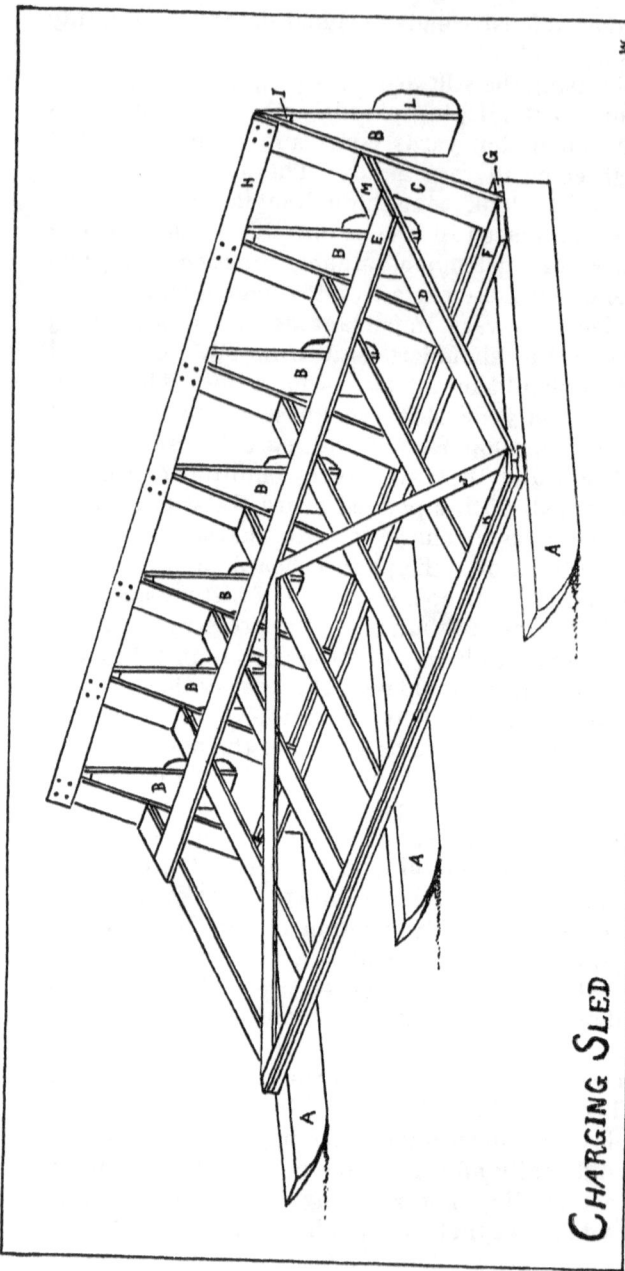

Charging Sled.—The above charging sled is made in the following manner: The runners marked A are about seven feet long and made of six-by-ten, or eight-by-eight-inch timbers. The runners of the end runners is sixteen feet. The seven charging surfaces, marked B, are equal distances apart along this sixteen-foot width and the bottom ends are about one foot eight inches from the ground. The bottoms of these charging surfaces are well padded, as shown at L, and are about eighteen inches in length. The timbers, B, to which the pads are attached, are two by ten inches, and the top of the sled is about five feet high. Timbers C and F are two by eight, and timbers H and D are two by six. The bottom and top of the three timbers at K are two by six, and the center piece between them, and also timbers J and G, are two by four. Timbers C and B are beveled at the top and a wedge, I, is placed as shown. Timbers C, B, and H are bolted together as shown. Nails will do for securing all other timbers in place. An extra piece is placed as shown at M, between E and B.

PRACTICE FIELD EQUIPMENT

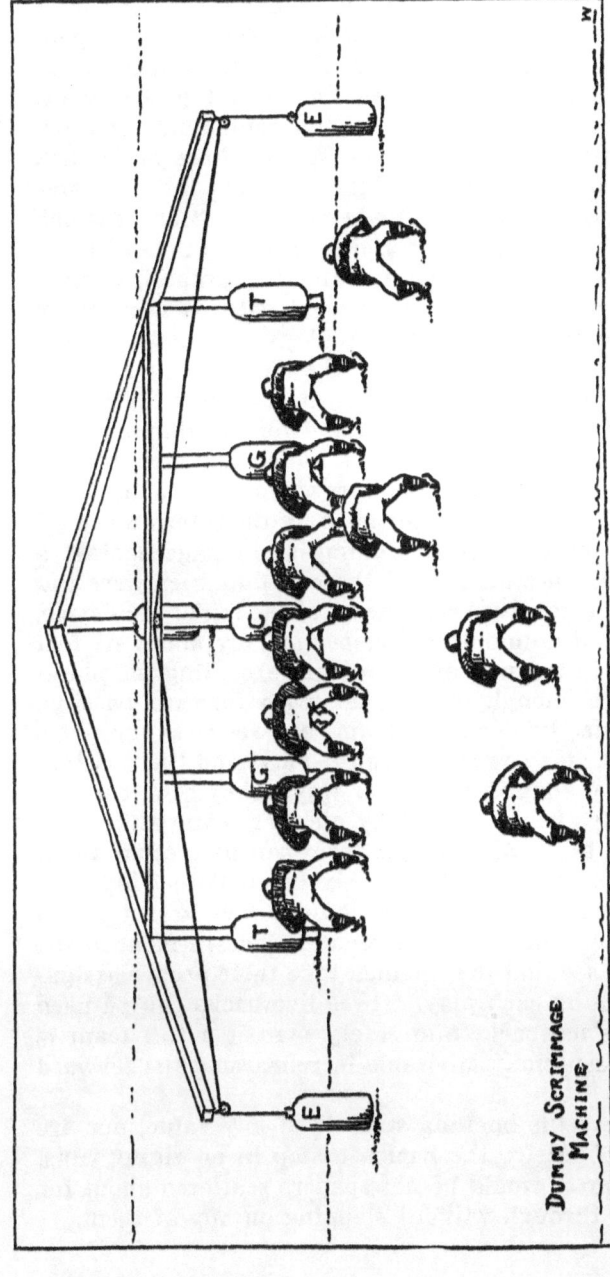

DUMMY SCRIMMAGE MACHINE

The above dummy scrimmage device is made in the following manner: The two outside posts representing the defensive tackles are timbers six inches square, placed twenty-one feet six inches apart from center to center. The three posts representing the center and guards are four inches square. These five posts are equal distances apart, set well in the ground, and are six feet high. The post representing the defensive fullback is six inches square, six feet high, and placed seven feet four inches directly back of the center post. Across the five posts representing the defensive line a timber four inches square is placed, and two timbers twenty-one feet six inches long and four inches square are placed from the fullback post over the tackle posts, extending out for supports for the end dummies. These timbers should be strong and might be a little larger if four-by-four timbers are not found of sufficient strength to withstand the strain of supporting the end dummies. All the posts are well padded from about three feet seven or eight inches high down to a few inches from the ground. Two pulleys are attached to the ends of the extending timber, and another is attached to the center of the timber across the line posts, through which a three-quarter-inch rope runs and supports the end dummies on either end. The center pulley is for preventing sag in this rope and keeping it out of the way of the players.

plays. This device would be especially valuable for the use of teams where the squad is small in number. There are five padded posts set well in the ground and at the same distances apart that players in a regular defensive line would probably be. These five padded posts represent the five center men of a defensive line. Another padded post is set about three yards back of the center of these five posts; this represents the defensive fullback, and affords a support for one end of the timbers which extend over the two outside posts and from which the defensive end dummies are suspended. These dummies can be just hung in place or, better still, can be connected with each other by means of a rope running through pulleys, as shown in the drawing. This arrangement allows the dummy ends to be blocked away from the play and downed, and they then automatically come back into place. These defensive dummy ends are suspended in about the position in which real ends will be met by the interference in a regular scrimmage, and, being movable dummies, they can be hit hard by the interference—a thing which cannot be done in dummy scrimmage against a real team, or could not be done if the end dummies were immovable padded posts. The cross pieces at the top of the device, from which the end dummies are suspended, are about six feet high and are not in the way of the men in executing the plays, nor are they high enough to interfere with forward passing.

With this device two or three teams can rehearse the plays alternately and the players can learn the plays and their assignments much better than in any other way. They also learn by watching the plays being run off by another team while they are waiting their turn. A small platform can be erected about fifteen yards back of the posts, say six or eight feet high, on which the head coach can stand or sit the better to watch and direct the practice. The line coach should stand in front of the offensive team to see that the linemen take their proper assignments in blocking on each play. Three live backs can be used for the defensive halfbacks and safety man if a full team is desired. This is especially advisable in rehearsing the forward pass plays.

I do not believe the bucking strap is of any value, nor are boxes scattered about for the backs to step in on zigzag runs. Better than the boxes would be newspapers scattered about for the backs to run through without stepping on any of them.

THE RUDIMENTS

I cannot stress too prominently the importance of a thorough mastery of such rudiments of football as tackling, blocking, falling on the ball, charging, punting, passing, and so forth. A team well coached and proficient in all the rudiments of the game will prove a hard team to beat even if the plays are not well conceived or well mastered. A great many coaches neglect the rudiments altogether too much and put their time and attention more upon learning some fancy or intricate plays. This is true of high-school more than of college coaches, the best of whom have become successful largely through their insistence on thorough basic training. High-school boys need rudimentary coaching and practice more than the college players because most of them are inexperienced and just learning the game. Yet the best college coaches devote more attention to schooling their charges thoroughly in the rudiments or fundamentals of football than do most high-school coaches. I have often been surprised by the ignorance of primary rudiments of the game shown by players who have perhaps just finished three or four years of high-school football. All coaches should realize that a team well grounded in the fundamentals, with a comparatively few simple plays thoroughly mastered, will prove much more successful than a team whose fundamental training has been neglected in order that more time could be devoted to learning an unnecessarily large assortment of plays.

TACKLING

Good, hard, sharp, and sure tackling is the very essence of a successful defense, and no player should hope to be placed upon a team unless he has become adept in this most important of football fundamentals. No team is going to be very severely beaten, even if it has no offense at all, if it is composed of eleven good tacklers, and coaches who include in their teams some players who are expert in some other department of play but who cannot tackle, are making a serious mistake.

Good tackling requires nerve. It means sustaining the shock of collision of two players meeting at top speed. But a good tackler realizes that such a collision takes more out of the man carrying the ball and hurts him more than it does the tackler himself, and sharp and fierce tackling has been the means of taking the zip and dash out of many star ball carriers to such an extent that they were greatly slowed up and rendered impotent. Nothing will take the pep and fight out of an opposing team or so discourage them as will fierce tackling. I have seen many a team start with snap and dash and power, looking like champions early in the game, only to be slowed up and tamed and eventually beaten by a supposedly weaker team whose players were vicious and relentless and sure tacklers. It is important then that this rudiment of play should be given first importance both by coaches in developing a team and by players who are anxious to make the team.

There are two distinct methods of tackling. One is with the shoulder, and is used wherever possible to meet a runner straight on or from the side where the impact is sure to knock the runner off his feet. It is also used in tackling from the rear. The other method is tackling from the side by throwing the body across the path of the runner and thus stopping his progress and forcing him to run into the tackler's arms. In this side tackle, the shoulder is not used to hit the runner but the head and shoulders are shot across the runner's path, the tackler at the same time turning his body so as to face the runner, hooking one arm sharply around the runner's outside knee, and with the other arm clasping both knees tightly together against the tackler's breast. In this or any other form of tackling the

SIDE TACKLING

tackler should not grasp the clothing or one leg in each hand, but rather should lock his hands around both legs of the runner. The start, contact, and finish of this form of tackling are shown in the drawing on another page. This method of tackling takes nerve because it involves the necessity of diving across the path of the runner, whose knees are seemingly dangerous; but injuries are seldom incurred in this form of tackling, and it is not as hard on the tackler as is the shoulder tackle. The player who lacks nerve or who has not been taught this method of tackling will attempt to stop a runner from the side by hitting him with the shoulder and with the head back of the runner, instead of in front. Then the tackler only has one arm to stop his man, and a strong runner with good knee action will tear loose from this one-arm grasp unless he has been knocked off his feet.

In developing this side tackle it should be apparent that the player must be given practice in tackling both to the right, in which case the tackler should turn on his right side as the runner is met and shoot his right arm sharply around the outside knee of the runner, and to the left, when it is necessary to turn the shoulders that way and hook the runner's outside knee or leg with the left arm.

The shoulder tackle is the natural method of tackling, and whenever it is possible to meet a runner straight on, or slightly to either side, or at any time when the tackler has to make a long or desperate dive to reach the runner, this method should be used. In making any tackle the player should be coached to crouch low, with shoulders near the ground, and to shoot the body forward with a powerful leg drive, keeping close to the ground. No tackler can get results by simply running up to the runner and then attempting to grab him. Such a tackler is easily warded off by the runner's free arm. The tackler must be low, and the body must be shot forward with speed and force so as to either get under the runner's stiff-arm or break it down. In tackling from the side or rear the tackler should leave his feet and dive for the runner, but in meeting a runner straight on the dive is not advisable. In such cases the tackler, if in the open field, should slow up just before reaching the runner so that he may change his course and tackle to either side if the runner attempts to dodge him. He should meet the runner with feet well braced so that the force of the runner will not carry

TACKLING

Straight-Ahead Tackling

him backward, and his feet should be well apart so that the runner will not veer to one side and lunge forward for a couple of yards' gain after being hit. If met squarely the runner's momentum, when he is suddenly stopped, will carry him off the ground, and the tackler can slam him back in no gentle manner. This form of tackling is also shown in the drawings on another page.

Tackling seems to come easily and naturally to some players, while others find it a difficult thing to learn. It is something like swimming in that it is difficult for some to learn at first but when learned it seems quite easy and is never forgotten, although great improvement can be made with continued practice and experience. Nothing shows up a player quicker than good or poor tackling. Critics, coaches, and spectators alike are sure to watch the progress of the ball, and therefore they note every attempt to stop the ball carrier. A good tackle or a missed tackle is always apparent to everybody watching the game. That practice and experience has a great deal to do with developing good tackling is proved by the fact that the best tacklers on almost every team are the ends and backfield men, which is largely due to the fact that these players have more tackling to do than do the five center linemen and therefore get to be more proficient in it. They learn by experience and practice how to ward off, sift through, or avoid interference, and these are important things for all tacklers to learn.

Tackling can be developed to a large extent by the use of the tackling dummy and by tackling each other. The shoulder tackle is too rough work to be much used on other players and for this reason the dummy is most useful for this practice. Side tackling can best be learned, and without danger of injury, by tackling each other, the runner standing facing at right angles to the tackler, or jogging slowly past him. The players should alternate in tackling and being tackled, and the tackling should be developed so that the players can bring the runner down with equal proficiency whether he is passing to the right or left.

Head-work, or the use of brains and judgment in tackling, is a very important consideration. The man carrying the ball has one arm free, and he probably is expert in using this free arm in warding off tacklers; therefore the tackler should remember that the runner will try to pass him on his free side.

TACKLING

It should be the aim of the tackler so to maneuver for position as to compel the runner to try to pass him on the side where his free arm will be of little use. The runner will also use his head; he will try to make the tackler think he is going that way anyway, and will endeavor to deceive him by dodging. He may also shift the ball to the other arm just before reaching the tackler. All these things should be watched, for generally a tackler can force the runner to try to pass him on the side he wishes.

A tackler should remember that, as a rule, a hard tackle hurts the opponent more than it does the tackler, and when met fiercely a few times a runner is inclined to slow up and try to save himself. On the other hand, if the tackler shows signs of fear or weakness, the runner will come at him more fiercely each time.

In practicing tackling, it is well to keep the hands closed so as to learn to depend upon the body and arms. Too often tacklers depend upon securing a grasp upon the runner's clothes or legs with their hands.

BLOCKING AND INTERFERENCE

Just as tackling is the most important feature of defensive play so is blocking and interfering the main thing in offensive football. The ball carriers cannot gain ground, no matter how clever they may be, if the opponents are not blocked out of the path of the runner, whereas a good blocking and interfering team can gain ground consistently with mediocre ball carriers. For this reason backs should be chosen for their blocking and interfering ability fully as much as for their ability to tote the ball. It is often found that a so-called star back, while clever at carrying the ball and avoiding tacklers, is practically useless in blocking and interfering. For that reason he may not be placed on the team, and his friends and the public, who have seen him getting away for clever runs, partly by his speed and sidestepping ability but mostly because the other backs cleared the way for him, wonder why he is not used more. Very often the coach is unjustly accused of favoritism in playing some back less clever at ball-carrying, instead of the "star." These people as a rule only see what a player does when carrying the ball and do not note what he is doing when the other backs are the ball carriers. The coach and critics, however, do note these things and no player should hope to make the team whose only real value on offense is in carrying the ball. I have seen halfbacks make the so-called All-American teams through publicity gained by making many long, clever runs when as a matter of fact those runs were made possible by the excellent interference provided by the other backs. If a "star" halfback does not make the team it is because he is weak in other departments of the game. Coaches are the ones most vitally interested in the success of their teams and they want the best men in the lineup.

It is important that not only all the backs be good blockers, but also the linemen must be adept in this most important of offensive duties. They must either charge and block in the line, go through and block off the secondary defense men, or leave their positions and come out as interferers leading and helping the backs to clear the opponents out of the path of the runner. They must block in opening holes in the line and they must block to protect the kickers. Thus on all running plays it is simply charge, block, and interfere for every man on the team except the man entrusted with the ball.

In the early days of the game all blocking and interfering was done with the shoulder and interferers seldom left their feet, but in recent years the body or Indian block, so named because the Carlisle Indians were the first to adopt it, has come into general use in blocking and interfering in the open field and to some extent in the line. The shoulder block is most used in blocking on the line and in opening holes for the runner, and is still used somewhat in the open field, but about the only time in the open field when shoulder blocking is preferable to the body or rolling block is where two interferers get to an opponent at the same time. For instance, it should be used when two men are designated to take out the defensive end and the play is so timed that these two men reach the end at about the same moment. If they leave their feet they would interfere with each other; therefore they should try to meet the opponent with their shoulders and catch him between them, as is illustrated on page 75 by drawings labeled "Double Teaming" or "Two on One." If, however, two men are delegated to take the defensive end and the play is so timed that one of the interferers gets to the end a step or two ahead of the other, the first man to meet the end should leave his feet and cut the end down with the whole length of his body while the other interferer, sometimes referred to as the clean-up man, bumps off the opponent with his shoulder as he is perhaps recovering from, or fighting off, the first man who hit him. The body or Indian block is preferable to the shoulder block in the open field because the blocker has the whole length of his body to throw across the path of the opponent, whereas with the shoulder block he only has the width of his shoulders and the opponent can rather easily turn the interferer to the side or dodge him. Then the interferer is tempted to throw out an arm to get his man, thus incurring a penalty. The interferer using the shoulder block is also inclined to half block a dangerous potential tackler and go on to block another man, whereas the first man met is the all-important opponent to get out of the way.

In the body block, besides having the whole length of the body to work with, the blocker is not tempted to use his hands, and in leaving his feet and cutting down his opponent, he is

BLOCKING

blocking a dangerous man effectively rather than being tempted to half block his primary assignment in the hope of continuing on and getting another man.

The Indian block, body block, or clipping block is made by the interferer leaving his feet, throwing his body at the opponent by turning the head and shoulders to one side, and whipping the legs around so that the opponent is hit just above or at the knees by the blocker's hip or the body just above the hip, the blocker trying to catch his man in the angle formed by his thigh and side. There is a sort of turning movement of the body and the blocker follows through by continuing this turning and rolling completely over. If the interferer turns his head and shoulders to the left he hits the opponent with the right leg extended, and as he follows through and the right knee hits the ground, the left leg is brought swiftly around and well extended. The contact is shown in the middle drawing on opposite page, and the lower drawing shows the blocker turning and bringing around his left leg. If the opponent is backing up or holding off the blocker, the turn is continued so as to keep the opponent going back. In this body blocking or clipping the interferer's head should as a rule be toward the opponent's goal if blocking to either side. In the drawings for instance it would have been more nearly correct if the blocker had hit the threatening tackler with his head to the right. Where one interferer is to take out the end on a play outside of tackle he should as a rule hit the end with his head toward the opponent's goal. This, however, cannot always be done, because the tackler may dodge to one side or the other of the oncoming interferer, and the interferer should turn his head and body to the side on which the tackler is trying to go.

The side-swiping body block is often used by the ends and wing backs in boxing a tackle in or out by the method commonly known as "high-lowing." For example, the play is going outside the opponent's left tackle. This tackle is standing outside of the offensive end, but may be flanked by a wing back. In this case the end dives low at the tackle's legs and the wing back hits him rather high with the shoulder and dumps him over the body of the end, as shown in Drawing 9 (page 75) illustrating the chapter on line play. If the play is to go inside of the left tackle the wing back hits the tackle low with his body and the end hits him high, as is shown in Drawing 10 on the same page.

The body block is also used by linemen as a follow-up of the shoulder block when the opponent has avoided the latter and is about to break through. For instance, the play is going to the right and the offensive center is delegated to block a certain opponent. He charges at him with his left shoulder, but the opponent, using his hands, deflects the center's charge so that the latter misses his man and has his head deflected to the right. The center then pivots and brings his right leg sharply around, thus either stopping his man or delaying him long enough so that he can do no damage to the play.

Shoulder blocking is done mostly in the line, in blocking opponents away from the play, and in opening holes. In this work a hard, low, quick charge is made and the blocker should get his head between the opponent and the play, except in double-teaming, in which case the blockers try to get the opponent with the inside shoulders and with their heads on the outside, as shown in Drawing 8 (page 75) illustrating the chapter on line play. If a play is going outside of tackle to the right, the blocking linemen should shoot their heads to the right of their opponents and block with the left shoulder. The exception is in the case of the right end if he has the help of a wing back in boxing the tackle, when he goes straight at the tackle and prevents the latter from making any advance while the wing back hits him on the outside and turns him in, both using the shoulder block or working the "high-low" on him. In opening a hole the two men who are to block their opponents away from the play should charge forward, the player on the left taking a step with his right foot and the man on the right with his left foot and shooting their heads between opponents and the play hole, hitting the opponents with the shoulder and pushing them back and to the side with the advanced foot. This is shown in Drawing 11 (page 75) in the chapter on line play.

In charging and blocking in the line too many players make one lunge and are all through, instead of making a sustained charge and keeping their opponent going back by following through as should always be done. Linemen also have a rather common fault of stopping and looking back to see what damage their opponent does when the latter succeeds in avoiding the block and getting by them. If an attempt at blocking fails the blocker should keep going and block off some secondary defense man, or at least keep out of the way of his own ball carrier. There is an old adage, and it is a good one to remember, that "A good interferer never looks back."

If opponents are using a standing line and straight-arm defense, the line may be broken rather easily if the offensive linemen have their heads and shoulders rather high and quickly duck as their charge is made. By this method the defense men's extended arms will shoot over the shoulders they jabbed at, and the offensive line, being under their men, can ride them out of the way very easily. In this way the Carlisle Indians used to handle the much heavier Harvard forwards with great success, because we knew that Harvard was wedded to that style of line defense.

FALLING ON THE BALL

The more open game has put a premium upon taking chances, and consequently the ball is fumbled a great deal more than it used to be when the rules encouraged conservatism and when only those plays were used in which there was little chance of a fumble. Consequently it is necessary to know how to fall on the ball and recover fumbles, notwithstanding the recent rule change which has made all passes except those from center to runner come under the same rule as forward passes, in that the ball cannot be lost by the side making the pass except on a fourth down. The direct pass from center to ball carrier is the method most commonly used in preference to the old quarterback or indirect pass method, and there will be fumbles as heretofore in thus getting the ball to the runner. Most fumbles are made after the runner has received the ball—usually when he is tackled or is grasped by the arm with which he is holding the ball, or when he falls and loosens his hold on the ball to protect himself. Therefore, although the danger of losing the ball on fumbles in passing the ball from one player to another has been eliminated, there will still be plenty of fumbles which create a free ball, and it is just as necessary as ever that all players become adept at recovering these fumbles.

Players should be able to drop on the ball on either side with equal ease, make running dives for it, and become accustomed to securing it under all sorts of conditions. Most players are used to dropping always on the same side when going after a fumble; but it is often advisable to drop on the other side. Unless the players have been given practice both ways they are likely not to fall the right way at times when they should throw their bodies between an opponent and the ball.

A player should not fall on the ball but rather around it, and he should not go after it with his hands, as many do when they first start practice. As mentioned above, the player should be able to drop on either side equally well. The ball should be covered as much as possible when the opponents are close at hand, so that none of them can get it away from the man falling upon it, or get their hands on it in such a way that the referee may think it belongs to them. If none of the opponents are near

FALLING ON THE BALL

FALLING ON THE BALL

enough to prevent the player gaining some ground after securing the ball, he should get to his feet as quickly as possible. Therefore it is advisable for the player to practice falling on the ball and rolling up on his feet. Practice will soon enable him to do this in remarkably quick time.

When an opponent is also endeavoring to fall on the ball, the player should throw himself between the opponent and the ball, and block him off with his back, as shown in the bottom illustration on page 43. If they are both running in the same direction after the ball, the blocking can be done before the dive for the ball is made.

Good judgment should be used as to when to fall on the ball and when to try to pick it up for a run. It should be remembered that getting the ball is the most important thing, while getting away with it for a run is secondary. No chances should be taken by trying to pick up a ball if opponents are at hand who might secure it first. If a fumbled ball is bounding so that it can be grasped in the air, that of course should be done, and where there are no opponents near with an equal chance to dive on the ball it can often be picked up with safety and profit. Care should be taken and practice should be had in picking up a loose ball while on the run. In such a case the ball should be scooped up from the side and not from directly in front of the runner, both because of the danger of kicking the ball forward and because scooping the ball up from the side is easier.

The illustrations show how a player should crouch low and dive for a loose ball, how he should drop with his forearm over but not on the ball, and how he should cover it and protect it in case he is not in the open where he can roll up on his feet for a run. The bottom drawing shows how a player's body should be thrown between an opponent and the ball, thus blocking him off or wresting the ball from him. In falling on the ball the players should be cautioned against hitting the ground with their shoulders, since many shoulder injuries have happened in this way.

PUNTING

Almost any player can acquire accuracy and fairly good distance in punting by practice and study of form, but the exceptionally good punters are born and not made and no amount of training and practice can make a great punter out of a player who does not have a natural ability to kick. This natural talent can be greatly developed by proper coaching and training and practice. Care should be taken that too much practice is not indulged in early in the season, as the leg is liable to become sore and lame for the same reason that a baseball player's arm so often goes wrong in early practice. It is no easy matter to get a leg into shape again when straining or overdoing has once got in its work. Do not try for distance the first week or two of practice, but devote attention to form and accuracy and to getting the kicking leg in good condition.

The spiral punt is universally used because a ball punted in this way goes farther, can with practice be punted more accurately, and is much harder to catch. In order to get the necessary distance and punt the spiral with accuracy, some practice should be devoted to it every day and great attention should be paid to form. It is correct form to hold the ball as far away from the body as possible, directly in front of the kicking foot, with one hand on each side of it or with the left hand somewhat farther forward than the right and the outer point of the ball slightly lower than the end nearest the body. The punter takes a short step forward with the kicking foot, then a regular step with the other foot, drops the ball so that it will fall as held, and meets it with the instep of the kicking foot about two and one-half feet from the ground. The toe of the foot should be extended and depressed and the leg should swing mostly from the hip and little at the knee, bringing the foot forward with a quick snap as the leg is straightened at the instant of contact. The punt should be followed out with the leg as far as possible and the body should bend backward so as to get the full weight of the player into the kick. The ball should be so dropped that its outer end will be somewhat lower than the other end when the foot meets it, and the long axis of the ball should be slightly at an angle from the flight of the ball, the forward end being a

Dropping the Ball for a Punt.

Meeting the Ball.

Follow Through

little to the left of this line, as shown in Drawing 2. At the moment of contact the foot should be swung a little to the inside, the spiral twist of the ball being imparted in this manner.

In punting from behind the line of scrimmage, the punter should regulate his distance from the center, from whom he receives the ball, according to the time he takes in getting off his punts and the ability of his team to prevent the opponents from getting to him. The ordinary distance is about ten yards. If the punter can add five yards to his punt by receiving the ball two or three yards farther back and taking more time it will pay to do it, as he not only gains two or three yards by so doing, but also gives his linemen more time to get down the field. The punter should not give the signal with his hands for the ball to be passed, as this enables the defensive team to charge on that signal instead of having to watch the ball.

The punter should try to place his punt as far away from the best handler of punts in the back field as possible. As soon as the ball leaves his foot he should always yell out "Right," "Left," or "Short," according to the direction or distance the ball is traveling, in order that the ends and other linemen may be directed quickly toward the spot where the ball is likely to land.

The velocity and direction of the wind should also be taken into consideration. If punting with the wind, the ball should be sent up higher into the air, as this will enable the wind to carry it farther down the field, and since it will be in the air longer the ends will have more time to get down under it. The ball should be driven low and hard against the wind.

A careful study of the illustrations will give valuable pointers in regard to correct form used by the best punters.

There are a few good punters who take only one step and these men can stand as near as eight yards from the ball with safety. The usual method is to take two steps, and if this is done the punter should be at least ten yards back. If three steps are taken it will be found advisable to be back twelve or more yards. The best method to teach is to have the punter stand back ten yards with his left foot slightly advanced and as the ball comes back he steps back easily with his left foot, completing the movement just as he receives the ball, then taking a short step with the right foot and a full step with the left.

Accuracy and consistency are more valuable assets for a punter than great distance. If a punter can place his kicks where he wants to he can keep the ball away from the safety man and he can often place the ball out of bounds for long gains and no possible return. In the opponent's territory, when a long punt might go over the goal line and result in a touchback, he should either place the ball out of bounds or kick it high enough so that his ends can get down the field and foul the ball before it rolls or bounds over the line.

The punter should be given plenty of practice in punting with men charging at him trying to block his kick, so that he will become accustomed to it. A punter who can kick sixty yards in practice with no one hurrying him but who gets off only an occasional good kick in the games is not an asset to a team. A consistent thirty-yard punter would be preferable.

In addition to distance, accuracy, and consistency, the punter must develop speed in getting off his kicks, and he should at all times keep his eye on the ball until it has left his foot.

A punter can practice too much, and care should be taken not to overwork the kicking leg. On Thursday the punters should ease up, and do no punting the day before the game.

JUDGING AND CATCHING PUNTS

In judging punts, the catcher should always have in mind the direction and velocity of the wind and the effect it will have upon the ball. He should regulate the distance he stands from the punter in accordance with this, together with the ability of the punter. These things need not be gone into fully, because any player of good common sense should have them always in mind and govern himself accordingly.

There is another thing to consider in judging punts which few players take into consideration, although a thorough understanding of this point will aid them greatly. This is the effect of the resistance of the air upon the course the ball will follow, and especially its effect upon spiral punts.

There are two kinds of spirals commonly punted—one in which the long axis upon which the ball revolves maintains the same relative position with regard to the ground throughout its course, and the other in which this axis gradually varies its position to follow the course of the ball, keeping its front end always pointed in the direction it is going, like the head of an arrow. If the ball were round the position of the axis on which it revolves would effect its course very little, but since a football is round one way and elliptical the other, the effect of the resistance of the air has a very marked influence upon its course, according to the position the ball maintains while traveling through the air.

It is obvious that the air resistance which the ball has to contend with is greater when the ball is traveling with its side or largest surface against the air in its path than it is when the ball keeps its end continually pointed in the direction of its course. In the latter case less surface is presented to the air, and consequently the ball will travel faster and farther.

The two kinds of spirals described travel through the first half of their course practically alike, and it is only in the last half, or after the ball begins to descend, that the difference in their position with reference to their course becomes apparent, and causes the air resistance to effect them differently. As explained above, the ball which keeps its front end pointed in the direction of its flight will carry farther because of less air resistance, but this is not the only reason for its longer flight. The ball in descending will tend to fall in the direction toward which its lower end points, since that is the direction or line of least resistance. Consequently, as shown in the diagram, the ball which maintains throughout its course the same position with reference to the ground will, in descending, not only meet more air resistance but will tend to slide down on the air in the direction pointed by its rear end, and will fall several yards short of where a round ball following a normal course (represented in the diagram by the solid line) would fall.

On the other hand, the ball which keeps its end or long axis pointed in the direction it is traveling presents its smallest possible surface to the air throughout its course, and consequently will travel faster and farther than will a round ball following a normal course.

The catcher should therefore watch the ball in its course and be governed in getting under it by the direction toward which its lower end is pointing while descending. When the spiral descends with its forward end nearest the ground, the catcher will understand that the ball will carry much farther than it will when it descends with its rear end inclined downward.

When the punt is judged correctly the catching of it is simply and easily accomplished, providing the player practices faithfully and has obtained a correct knowledge of how catching is done, either by being properly coached or by studying out the best method himself.

I have observed a great many coaches teaching their backs to catch punts by forming a sort of pocket with their arms,

Catching a Punt

Easing it Down

Pinning it to the Body

body, and the thigh of one leg, into which the ball is supposed to fall and be held by the arms. I believe this method is not the best form, and that very few players catch punts that way even when coached to do so. My observation and experience have convinced me that the best, simplest, and surest method of catching punts is simply to pin the ball to the body with the hands the instant it lands there. The hands should be extended toward the ball as it is descending, so as to come down to the body with the ball, and no attempt should be made to catch the ball with the hands alone except in cases where the ball has to be caught very close to the ground or above the head.

As the ball nears the catcher the latter's arms are well extended to meet it, one hand being extended somewhat farther than the other. Both hands guide or ease the ball down to the body, the hand farthest extended coming down on top of the ball and the other hand under it.

An important fact to remember in catching punts is that the eyes should not leave the ball for an instant until it is caught. Many punts are fumbled because players take their eyes off the ball an instant to see where the opposing ends are, and in what direction to run. This habit usually proves disastrous. While watching the ball descend, the catcher can usually see out of the corner of his eye where his opponent's ends are and in what direction he had better start. But whether he can or not, the catching of the ball is the all-important matter to attend to first, the running of it back being a secondary consideration.

When the punt has been caught, unless it is a fair catch, the ball should be quickly placed under the arm, and the player should start quickly and at top speed toward the opponent's goal. No time should be wasted in looking for an opening or in dodging back and forth across the field. Usually the best plan is to shoot straight ahead. Dodging back and forth looks pretty, and eluding several tacklers may create a little enthusiasm among the spectators who know little about the game, but the opposing forces are gathering all the time and such tactics usually result either in no gain or in a loss, and the player is not raised any in the estimation of the coach or of those who understand and appreciate good football. When the punt is caught there should be no hesitation and no giving of ground to elude a tackler.

PLACE-KICKING

Place-kicking has always been a very important feature of football because it has been used for goal kicking after touchdowns as well as for kicking goals from the field, and every team has had to develop one or more place-kickers. Until recently goal kicking after touchdowns was accomplished without much danger of being rushed or the kick being blocked, because the opponents were restrained behind their goal line until the ball was placed upon the ground. The holder of the ball had plenty of time to adjust the ball in a perfect position for the kicker, and the kicker could take his time without much fear of having his kick blocked. In recent years the try for goal after touchdowns had to be made from scrimmage formation so that speed in placing the ball and in kicking had to be developed, but goal kicking was still rather an easy task, because of the kick being permitted directly in front of the goal posts and only a short distance away. This year the rules have been so changed that tries for goals after touchdowns will be much more difficult because the goal posts are moved ten yards back of the goal line on the end zone line, and therefore goal kickers will have the mark they are to shoot at just ten yards farther away, which means that the ball must be kicked from a spot about twenty yards in front of the goal posts instead of about ten yards as has been the practice the past couple of years. This is assuming that the ball is kicked from a spot between six and seven yards behind the line of scrimmage.

It can easily be seen then that good place-kickers are going to be of greater service than ever before and it can also be seen that place-kickers who can get distance as well as accuracy in their kicks will be great assets to their teams. Goals from the field are rendered increasingly hard for the reason that the goal is farther away. A place-kick when the ball is put in play on the twenty-five-yard line, assuming that the kicker kicks from about seven yards behind the line, must now clear the bar at a distance of forty-two yards away, and that is a very difficult assignment for even the best of place-kickers.

The place-kick is much easier to develop than the drop-kick and more generally used, both for kicking goals from the field

PLACE-KICKING

and for goal kicking after touchdowns. Only in rare instances when a player has developed very unusual skill in drop-kicking is it advisable to use that method in preference to the place-kick.

In place-kicking the ball must be kicked from a point so far back of the scrimmage line that the opposing ends cannot get in to block the kick even though they are unobstructed, or from a point so near the line that the opposing ends cannot get in front of the ball. This is because it is almost impossible to block off both the opposing ends and tackles. Place-kicks from a point from seven to ten yards back of the line are the hardest to protect and the most easily blocked, and now that place-kicks must be ten yards longer to reach their mark it seems doubly advisable to kick the ball from a spot as near the line of scrimmage as possible. Six yards will be found to be about the correct distance because this is far enough back so that the ball can be raised over the scrimmage line, and near enough to prevent the opposing ends from getting in behind the two backs who are protecting the kicker and then changing their course to get in front of the ball. The line must play very close together and the protecting backs must force the opposing tackles to go outside of them, and if no opponent comes through the center of the line there will be no danger of the kick being blocked.

The holder of the ball should select as favorable a spot as he can find at a distance of about six yards directly back of the center, or on a straight line from the center and the goal if the ball is to be kicked from a position not directly in front of the goal posts. He should make a mark on the ground showing the kicker just where he will place the ball and then he should get into position to receive the ball from the center. He should be to the right of the kicker if the latter is right-footed and he should kneel on his left knee with his right foot on the ground toward the line in such a position that his body will be firmly and steadily supported, as shown in the illustration, or he may prefer to kneel on both knees. When he and the kicker are ready he should extend his arms toward the snapper-back, but he should give no signal for the ball because the defensive team could then charge upon his signal instead of having to see the ball put in play. It is best not to have any signal at all for the ball to be passed on this play, but rather let the center make the pass when he sees that the man who is to hold the ball and the man who is to kick are ready.

Upon receiving the ball from the center the holder should quickly place it in an upright position upon the exact spot he has previously marked, the left hand being withdrawn as soon as the ball is placed correctly and the fingers of the right hand holding the ball on top until just an instant before the kicker's toe comes in contact with it. It is not advisable to waste any time in rotating the ball so that a seam is toward the kicker, but if this can be done without loss of time it may be a little better, although it should make little if any difference in the accuracy of the kick.

Receiving and placing the ball for a kick is a very important part of successful place-kicking and should be practiced fully as much as the place-kick itself.

The kicker should stand with his feet together a little less than a yard back of the spot where the ball is to be placed and with the toe of his kicking foot on a direct line with the spot the holder has marked and the goal. He should then watch the ball from the time it leaves the center's hands until after the kick is made, and pay no attention whatever to the opponents who are trying to block the kick. The instant the ball is placed he should step forward with his left foot to a spot about eight inches from the ball and then kick with the right foot, hitting the ball as low as possible so as to raise it well in the air. If the kick is made from such a distance from the goal that great power is required, the kicker should stand a little less than two yards back of the ball and take two steps before the kick, making his first step with the kicking foot.

The distances I have mentioned are only approximate and vary with the height and stride of the kicker and the amount of power he must put into his kick.

Place-kickers often try to raise the ball by elevating their kicking toe an instant before contact and in this way they meet the ball so high off the ground that the exact opposite of the desired result is obtained. The toe should be depressed almost to the extent that the kicker seems to be kicking at a point on the ground just under the ball. In other words he should aim to drive his toe exactly between the ball and the ground.

Some kickers prefer to have the holder incline the ball

so that it is leaning toward the kicker, and others prefer to have it leaning away from them and toward the goal, but quickness in placing the ball is so important that it is best to place the ball in an upright or perpendicular position since this is the easier way and the method generally used.

Successful place-kicking necessitates protection of the kicker, accurate passing by the center, quick and skillful placing of the ball by the holder, as well as coolness and cleverness on the part of the kicker, and the play needs much practice by the whole team against opposition.

The formation and blocking on this play are shown and explained on page 186.

DROP-KICKING

Place-kicking is so much easier for coaches to develop, so much easier for the players to learn, and is so much more certain of success, that I never encourage players to practice drop-kicking. In drop-kicking the ball has to be dropped to the ground instead of being placed there by another player, and in dropping the ball it must strike the ground directly upon its end, or long axis, and must be in an upright or perpendicular position just as it hits. It stands to reason that another player, in the proper position, can receive the ball from the snapper-back and place it much more accurately and easily than the kicker can catch it, adjust it in his hands, and drop it. Not only that, but the holder of the ball for a place-kick can mark the spot on the ground where he is to place the ball and the kicker can get his proper stance and aim before the ball is passed, and he can concentrate his entire attention upon the one act of kicking instead of having to figure also upon catching the pass, adjusting it in his hands, aiming, and dropping the ball. In place-kicking the kicker sees the ball in position to kick, and he can vary his speed according to the time he has to kick and accommodate his aim to the ball in case the placer has not put the ball upon the exact spot which he marked.

In a drop-kick, timing is one of the most important things to accomplish, and one of the hardest to acquire. The toe has to meet the ball the instant the ball hits the ground. The difference of a fraction of a second means success or failure. This factor is eliminated in the place-kick, because the ball is placed on the ground and remains there until it is kicked, instead of rebounding as in a drop-kick.

I have heard coaches arguing that the drop-kick is faster than the place-kick, but I have tried both methods, timing players skilled in both, and I have satisfied myself that the place-kick can be gotten off just as quickly as the drop-kick.

About the only advantage the drop-kick has over the place-kick is that it permits a better triple-threat situation in that the kicker receives the ball and he can either kick, or fake a kick and forward pass, or run, better than can be done from a place-kick formation, and the kicker has one more man to protect him on his kick.

Occasionally a player may have developed a very exceptional and almost uncanny skill in drop-kicking, and it would be a mistake not to make use of that skill in the games.

Some coaches encourage the practice of drop-kicking, and nearly all players delight in practicing this scientific and spectacular stunt. Hence this book would not be complete without a description and explanation of proper drop-kicking form.

Drop- Kicking

There are different ways of holding the ball as it is dropped, some players preferring to hold it with one hand near the top and the other near the bottom. But the simplest and best way is to hold it directly between the hands. Some prefer to hold the lacing toward them, and others hold it with the lacing toward the goal. Either way is all right. The ball should be held in a perpendicular position as near the ground as the player can hold it and do his kicking, and it should be held directly in front of the kicking toe. If the kick is to be a short one, the kicker should stand with his feet together and with his body bent slightly forward. He should catch the pass, take a short step forward with the left foot, drop the ball, and kick with the right foot, the latter just skimming the ground, with the toe elevated just at the instant of impact with the ball. If rather long distance is required a short step with the right foot and a longer one with the left should be made. The kicker should be well back or well protected, because a drop- or place-kick is more easily blocked than a punt for the reason that the ball is kicked from the ground, whereas the punted ball starts from nearly a yard off the ground.

In drop-kicking it is very important that the kicker keep his eyes on the ball from the time it leaves the center's hands until it leaves his foot, and he should pay no attention whatever to the opponents who are charging through to block the kick. Much practice should be had in drop-kicking with men charging at the kicker, to accustom him to actual playing conditions. Some drop-kickers are wonderful performers in practice with no one bothering them, but it is only the cool-headed and nervy ones, who kick as well in games as in practice, who are of any value to a team.

Unless a player shows special skill in drop-kicking, coaches will do well to have the kickers confine their practice to place-kicking and punting. The timing and the dropping of the ball are altogether different in punting and in drop-kicking, and it does not do the punters any good to practice the latter.

KICKING OFF

The rules committee has made it unlawful to tee up a ball for goal kicking or for place-kicking. When there was no rule against it, time was wasted by players building up needlessly high tees, sometimes going to another part of the field to gather up mud or clay for the purpose. Some teams had tees already built up of clay and placed where they could find them near the side or goal lines. The rules committee was fully justified in trying to cure the evil, but I do not think it was necessary or advisable to prohibit teeing up altogether. There could be no harm in players scraping up what loose dirt is within easy reaching distance of the ball, so as to enable them to make the ball stay in position while kicking and to raise it slightly from the surrounding ground. This would result in better kicking and would save time, because without any loose dirt to support it the ball is hard to make stand on end on smooth or hard ground and a needless amount of time is sometimes required to make the ball stay put. I hope the committee will remedy the situation some time in the near future by permitting a small tee to be made of what loose dirt can be scraped up, say within one yard of the ball.

In placing the ball for the kick-off it is nearly always necessary for the kicker to make a depression in the ground with his heel. He should not do this if he can make the ball stand without so doing and, if the kicker has difficulty in raising the ball on the kick, he should have a team mate hold the ball in position rather than set it in a depression. It is usual to have one player of the kicking side stay back as safety man on the kick-off, and this man can be utilized for holding the ball. Some kickers prefer to have the ball straight up, others like it leaning away from them, and still others can kick better with the ball leaning a little toward them. The players preferring to have the ball leaning one way or the other should certainly have the ball held for them, while the man using the upright ball can usually place the ball so that it will stand without holding.

After seeing that the ball is placed to suit him, the kicker should go back a few yards, depending on how much of a run he requires, and when the referee blows his whistle start his run slowly until he feels that his step is coming right and then go at full speed, striking the ball as close to the ground as possible so as to raise it in the air. The kick-off man should practice whenever he has the opportunity so that he can not only raise the ball high and secure good distance, but can also place his kicks accurately. The team receiving the kick-off usually has its best runner directly in front of the goal, and it is generally an advantage to place the kick-off to either side of the gridiron, the kicker notifying his team-mates which side he is to kick to so that they may have their best men on that side or perhaps have more men there. If the ball is kicked out of bounds at the first trial, no chances should be taken on the second kick by trying to kick it to the side.

FORWARD PASSING

The forward pass, a bastard offspring of real football, has come to be a very important and popular part of the game. I have always believed that the legalizing of forward passing was a mistake, and I still think so. When the rules committee, in response to the demand of the public years ago for reforms tending to make the game safer for the players and more interesting to the spectators, cut out pushing and pulling of the runner, thus making ground gaining harder, and at the same time increased the distance to be gained for a first down to ten yards instead of five, something had to be done to make ground gaining easier. Some method of scattering the defense so that running plays could not be stopped so easily was considered the best solution of the problem, and two ways of trying to force the secondary defense to play well back of the line were tried. The forward pass, under certain restrictions, was introduced into the game, and the on-side kick was given a trial. In the latter case the side kicking the ball was allowed to secure possession of it after the kicked ball hit the ground. This resulted unsatisfactorily because it introduced into the game a method of play which put a premium upon having the ball rolling around on the ground instead of being cleanly handled, and the on-side kick was soon put into the discard and the forward pass was concentrated on as the best method of forcing the secondary defense to play well back of the line where they were at some disadvantage in stopping running plays, but in a position to defend against the pass. Right there I believe is where the rules committee made a mistake. The on-side kick was unsatisfactory because before the kicking side could secure the ball it had to hit the ground. This could easily have been corrected if the rule had been changed so that the players of the side kicking the ball could have caught the kick just as they now do a forward pass. What prettier play could there be than to have the ball punted accurately to a spot unguarded by the defense and having an end on the punter's team dash down the field and catch the punt for a long gain?

This would have been real football and it would have solved the problem by legitimate football methods instead of by a method theretofore entirely foreign to the game. It had been a basic theory in the sport that football was a game in which the ball was advanced by either rushing or kicking, and basketball tactics had no part in the game. The big objection to the forward pass is the large number of incompletions which result in no plays and which force the officials to carry the ball back and forth about as much as the two teams. This could have been entirely overcome by legitimatizing and regulating the on-side kick, and every play could have been a play whether the punt was caught or not.

Some critics might argue that this would have put a premium on an overdose of kicking, but the rules could have stipulated that the defense would have the first right to secure a kicked ball by signaling for a fair catch if he could handle the ball, and if the man so signaling failed to get under the ball, then the offensive team would be given the ball where it hit the ground. That would have prevented signaling for a fair catch to keep the offensive team from trying to catch the ball unless the back signaling was sure he could get to it. The object of the kicker, of course, would have been to place the kick out of reach of an opponent and where his own man could catch it, and if this was not done, then the defensive team could have fair-caught the ball. There would have been no collisions such as now occur when opponents are trying to get a pass. Accuracy of punting would have been developed and the game would have been all football. There would have been no permitting punts to hit the ground purposely to make it anybody's ball. The object of forcing the secondary backs to play well back of the line would have been gained, because if the halfbacks were up close to the line a short punt could be placed down the center or off to one side over the halfback's head but too short for the safety man to handle, and an offensive end could run down and take it out of the air for a long gain.

For these reasons I claim that the forward pass was unnecessary and the on-side kick could have been legitimatized and regulated in such a way as to have served the purpose for which the forward pass has been legalized, and the game would have been just as spectacular as it is now, and much more satisfactory. I hope that some day this change will be made.

Mistake or no mistake, the pass is with us and it has not

only become popular and spectacular, but it has also come to be one of the most important of weapons in the hands of offensive teams who can make the most of its use. It is becoming more and more effective as its possibilities are becoming better known through experience and scientific development. Considered more as a threat than as an effective weapon of offensive football in the early days of the pass, this play is each year being used more and more as a regular ground-gaining play. Within a few years the rules committee will have to curb its use by further rules to prevent it from dominating the game at the expense of rushing and kicking the ball and to keep the game from being considered as "passball" instead of football.

There are several kinds of forward passes, referred to as overhand passes, underhand passes, side-arm passes, long passes, short passes, lob passes, end-over-end passes, and spiral passes. The spiral overhand pass is the one most used and the one most effective for long distance and swift passing, because distance and speed and accuracy can best be obtained by this method and also because passes usually have to be made over the heads and upraised hands of opposing players who are hurrying the passes and attempting to knock down the pass, and the overhand pass is much harder to block than is the side-arm or underhand pass. In making the overhand spiral pass the form is much the same as in throwing the javelin or spear. The ball is firmly grasped, with the ends of the fingers on the lacing to afford a better grip and to give something for the fingers to cling to in imparting the spiral to the ball. The grip is made and the ball is held by the fingers and thumb, and in getting a firm grip the other hand is used to help place the ball and to press it firmly into the throwing hand. The ball is usually gripped just back of its center, and when the arm is brought forward over the shoulder the ball is pointed in the direction of flight, the palm of the hand is held upward, and at the moment the ball is leaving the hand, the hand is whipped slightly to the left (if a right-handed passer) and the ball is made to rotate by loosening up with the thumb and allowing the ball to roll off the fingers, the finger tips being the last to be released from the ball. The correct form of this pass is shown in the drawings, the first showing the passer getting ready and placing the ball firmly in his passing hand, the next two showing him in the middle of this throw, and the fourth showing the finish, just after the ball has left his hand.

Nearly all players, except perhaps those with unusually small hands or short fingers, can learn with practice to throw the spiral pass with accuracy and for fairly good distance, but the players with big hands and long fingers are the boys who are best adapted to this department of the game. They can get a better grip on the ball and can control the throw much better than can their short-fingered brothers. Since the accuracy, distance, and speed attained by the passer counts for so much in successful forward passing, a team which has in its makeup a

THE FORWARD PASS.

1. GETTING READY.
2. THROWING (a)
3. THROWING (b)
4. THE FINISH.

passer who has those three qualifications is very fortunate and can make great use of this play. On the other hand, a team which has only mediocre passers cannot hope to make much of a success of their passing attack.

Bullet-like swiftness of the pass is advisable for distance passing, because a high, slow pass gives the defensive men more time to get under it. Swift passes are also used for shorter distances when there are no players between passer and receiver. The lob pass is used for short or medium length passes when the ball has to be passed over a defensive player's head or over masses of players, and is suitable for use on screen passes or on short flank passes. Where speed is not essential and there is not much danger of interception, short lob passes are preferable because they are easier caught by the receiver, who can quicken or slacken his speed, or vary his course, to get under the ball. Speedy passes must be very accurate to reach their mark.

Deception on the part of the passer is a very important part of successful forward passing, and the passer should conceal as much as possible the fact that he is going to pass. When it becomes apparent to the defense that a pass is coming, the passer should conceal the direction of his throw by looking or feinting to a decoy and then quickly whipping the ball to the real receiver. The passer should not be compelled to locate his man, but should know just where the receiver is to be, so that he can almost connect with the receiver without looking in that direction at all. Good faking or theatricals on the part of forward passers is a feature which helps very greatly in a forward passing attack, and it has not been developed by most coaches and passers to the extent that is advisable.

With the lateral pass encouraged as it now is by the new rules, ball carriers are going to acquire more generally the habit of carrying the ball in front of them in both hands, instead of placing it under an arm, so that they may always be ready to flip the ball to another player when about to be tackled. This method of carrying the ball is going to aid in forward passing because there will be more deception as to whether or not the back so carrying the ball is starting off for a run or is going to make a forward or a lateral pass. Deception of this kind, the passer starting off tackle as if for a run, and then quickly veering back and making his throw, is a method which will increase in use and will pay dividends. Faking the ball to a player for a line buck and then running back to pass is a favorite and effective method of deception employed by teams which use a quarterback to handle the ball. Another favorite method of deceiving the opponents as to whether or not a pass or run is being attempted is for the passer to receive the ball from another player as though for a reverse play. By these methods the defense is drawn in to stop the supposed running play and their attention is distracted from the pass receiver, who has more time to get into position because the pass is somewhat delayed. The receiver can allay any suspicion that he is going after a pass by blocking in the line before dashing for an unprotected spot.

A good thing for coaches to emphasize, and for passers to remember, is the advisability of passing plenty far—to over-pass the receiver rather than to under-pass him. The pass should be made so that the receiver has to extend himself by swift running and by jumping in the air to get it. Disastrous interceptions of passes usually occur when the passes are too short and the receivers have overrun them. If the pass is too long and is intercepted, the receiver is right in front of the man who has intercepted the pass and can easily down him. Then, too, the most successful passes are the ones wherein ball and receiver just barely connect while the receiver is on the dead run, or when he has to go high in the air to pull the ball down. On the other hand, passes are rarely successful when the receiver has to slow up or turn back to get the ball. By all means, therefore, encourage the passer to be sure to pass the ball far enough, and get after the receiver for being too slow if he fails to reach the ball.

CATCHING FORWARD PASSES

Most forward passes have to be taken and caught by receivers who are running in the same direction as the ball is coming, or with their side to the ball. In such cases the ball cannot be caught as a punted or kicked ball is handled, because in handling kicks the player is facing the ball and can catch it against his body. Forward passes, as a rule, have to be caught with the hands and arms alone and with the catcher's back or side to the ball. Pass receivers should be given plenty of practice taking passes at full speed and jumping in the air for them, and they should be taught not to look around for the ball until it is almost to them. For a runner to look back over his shoulder while running slows him up and helps the defense to know the real receivers from the decoys sent down the field. Sometimes a pass receiver will only be able to reach the ball with one hand and ease it down into his arms, but whenever possible he should use both hands on the ball. In catching the pass the body should be turned as little as possible, the receiver simply turning his head to get his eyes on the ball. The correct form is shown by the drawings.

I have called attention to the importance of deception on the part of the passer. This is also a very important feature for pass receivers and decoys to develop. Successful forward passing

Catching the Pass

depends as much upon the decoys as upon the real receiver, and good deception on the part of decoys should therefore be stressed very strongly. A decoy who half-heartedly deploys into position and by his careless manner, lack of speed, and failure to look around for the ball shows an alert defense that he is not the real receiver of the pass is entirely useless as a decoy and might better be used to help protect the passer. The real receiver should use deception to fool the man who is delegated to cover him, either by stopping momentarily to block an opponent before getting into position, or by quickly changing his course while passing his man. If these methods are not used the receiver must depend upon his speed in outrunning his man or upon a team-mate's decoying the man away from him. The right end who is to take a deep pass over to his side of the field should run straight down, pass the halfback on the inside, and then quickly veer off to the right. The halfback who turns to follow him will very likely turn to his own right or toward the receiver. Since he must make a complete turn, the halfback will probably find himself several steps behind the end, who, if the pass is accurately placed, can take it without opposition. This situation is mentioned to give an illustration of how best to deceive the defense by a quick change of course. If the end turned to the right before reaching the back, the latter could easily cover him.

If it is apparent to the receiver that a defensive player is going to be at the spot where the pass must be handled and will have a chance to catch or bat down the ball, the receiver should turn his body in such a way that he will block off the opponent at the same time that he is attempting to catch the pass.

After the pass is caught, the ball should quickly be placed under the arm while the receiver continues his course as far as possible toward the opponent's goal.

Long passes, if completed, result in long gains without any run; but they are harder to complete than short passes, and the latter are generally so planned that there is a good chance for a run after receiving them. For that reason it is desirable that ends should be able to advance and run in the open field. They should be given practice and experience in running with the ball along with the backfield players instead of being limited to practice in simply catching passes.

THE LATERAL PASS

Many attempts have been made by coaches to make use of the lateral or rugby pass in the years gone by. But such passes rarely proved to be of much value, and this method of advancing the ball was not considered practical until the recent rule changes whereby fumbles and incompletions of the pass have been made less dangerous, in that the ball cannot be recovered and retained by the opponents.

Heretofore the danger of losing the ball by fumbles or incompletions of the lateral pass was too great to overcome its advantages. The change in the rules does not make lateral passing any easier to accomplish, but since the danger of losing the ball on fumbles and bad passes on the play has been removed, lateral passing will become an interesting and valuable feature of offensive football. The coaches who prove to be the quickest to develop this feature and the cleverest in making use of its wonderful possibilities are going to have a considerable advantage over the more conservative mentors who are slow in adding this feature to their offensive systems of play.

Defensive ends are going to have doubly hard tasks in stopping flank runs because plays will be developed with one back carrying the ball apparently for a run inside the defensive end, but with another player deploying out beyond the end to whom the ball carrier can toss the ball by a lateral pass if the end comes in to tackle him. With clever backs, who know when to pass and when to continue without passing, and who at times may make clever fakes to pass, the ends are going to have a tough time defending their positions. Ball carriers will be coached to attempt to toss the ball to another player, if possible, when tackled or about to be tackled, and punt catchers and catchers of kick-offs will have excellent opportunities to flip the ball to team-mates farther out, when opponents converge upon them to stop their progress.

Lateral passes are made by tossing the ball to the side with both hands or with one hand. If one hand is used for the pass it should be the hand on the opposite side from which the pass is to be made; a pass to the right being made with the left hand, and to the left with the right hand. At times the passer will turn and face the man to whom he is passing, and in such cases the two-handed push pass used in basketball will come in handy. Care will have to be taken that the receivers of lateral passes are well back of the passer, because it can easily be seen that when a pass of a few feet is being made between players running down the field parallel to each other and an equal distance from the goal, such a pass, while lateral as between the players themselves, would actually be a forward pass because the receiver would have advanced somewhat from the line on which the passer stood when the ball left his hands.

Long lateral passes well across the field will be made with the overhand spiral throw, the same as forward passes; but such passes are not likely to prove practical except perhaps upon returning the kick-off.

The reasons why lateral passing never gained much headway in the American game were, first, as has been stated, because of the danger of losing the ball on a fumble or a bad pass, and second, because in the American game it has been advisable to utilize as many men as possible in the interference, to go ahead of the runner and clear the way for him, and men could not be spared from the interference to follow up or to flank the runner. In rugby no interference was legal and there was nothing for team-mates to do but to follow up the ball carrier or deploy to either side of him to be in a position to receive the pass. In the American game it has always been quite customary, however, to assign one man the duty of following up the play as a sort of safety man to guard the runner from behind and especially to watch for fumbles. This man can easily be utilized as the receiver of lateral passes under the new rules without weakening the interference.

The customary and correct method of carrying the ball has heretofore been to place it under one arm and carry it with one arm free, except on line bucks when it was advisable to have both hands on the ball. With lateral passing coming into favor we will become accustomed to seeing the ball carried out in front of the body in both hands, as it is in rugby, so that the carrier may be ready to make a backward or lateral pass.

In addition to the advantages of using the lateral pass as a method of ground-gaining, the new rules will remove a great deal of the danger involved in executing double- and triple-pass plays, and these are likely to be used more than when the ball was likely to be lost by fumbling in making these passes.

LINE PLAY

Although there follows a discussion of how to play each individual position, there are certain fundamentals common to all players or groups of players. Those which pertain particularly to line play, and which apply to all linemen, will be set forth here.

One of the most important fundamentals of line play, both on offense and defense, is the stance. Illustrating this chapter are drawings, showing correct stances, both offensive and defensive, for all linemen except offensive center; and a study of these drawings, together with the following descriptions, should enable any coach or lineman to teach or assume a proper position for the work which has to be done in the line.

The offensive stance is the same for all linemen except the center. The rules provide that both hands, or both feet, or one hand and the opposite foot, shall be within one foot of the scrimmage line. Some coaches teach their linemen to have both hands on the ground on the offense and the feet well back. This is a good stance for straight-ahead charging and might be used for all the linemen who do not come out for interference, but it is an awkward stance for interfering linemen. A better stance for all purposes is to have one foot about twelve to fifteen inches farther front than the other, and the feet about eighteen inches apart, with the hand opposite the advanced foot resting on the ground and supporting part of the weight of the body, the other forearm or hand being on the knee. The hips should be low and the back straight, and the player should be facing directly toward the opponent's goal. A good way to teach such a stance is to stand the linemen in line, with feet eighteen inches apart. Then have them all step back about a foot with the right foot and squat down as low as they can, so that they appear to be sitting on their heels, with the left forearm or hand resting upon the left thigh or knee. They then bring their shoulders forward, or fall forward until some weight rests upon the right hand, which is placed on the ground in front of the right foot and about eight inches farther forward than the toe of the left foot. Both feet should be pointing as nearly straight forward as is comfortable for the player. Such a stance is well illustrated in

LINE PLAY

1. STANCES — OFFENSIVE AND DEFENSIVE END AND TACKLE

2. DEFENSIVE GUARD AND CENTER

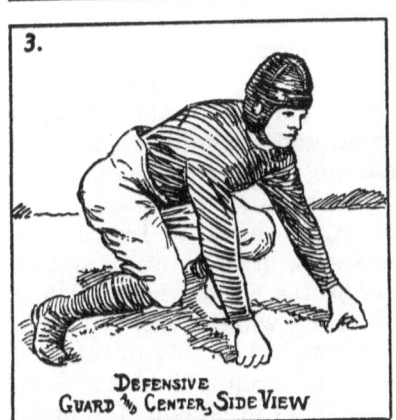

3. DEFENSIVE GUARD AND CENTER, SIDE VIEW

4. DEFENSIVE TACKLE

5. SIDE VIEW, OFFENSIVE GUARD

6. SAME, FRONT VIEW.

Drawing 1, showing stances, or in Drawings 5 and 6; but in the last two drawings the right foot is forward and left hand on the ground. Both ways of standing (left foot forward and right foot forward) should be practiced until the players can assume either position easily and naturally. If an offense is used in which none of the linemen come out in the interference, a stance such as is shown in Drawings 2 and 3 would be good. Linemen should have their feet well apart so that they will always be in a position to withstand charges from the side.

Having assumed a proper stance, the most important duties of linemen are either to charge and block, and open holes, or to come out of the line and interfere for the ball-carriers. Therefore linemen should be adepts in all the forms of blocking explained in a chapter under that head. In charging and in blocking in the line the shoulder block is most used, while in coming out in the interference, and also in going through and blocking in the open field, the body or rolling block is more often advisable. In blocking in the line a lineman should always try to get his head between his man and the play when he is handling a man alone. If he is assisting another lineman, working the two-on-one block, the opponent should be caught between the heads of the two blockers, as shown in Drawing 8. The method called high-lowing as shown in Drawings 9 and 10 is seldom used by any linemen except the ends, who employ it in working on the tackles with flanking wing backs.

The most common faults of linemen, in blocking in the line, are that they charge too high and do not keep under their men, and that they do not follow through. They are inclined to make one lunge, hit their opponents, and then fail to keep contact with them as they should. They should make what is called a sustained block if their opponents are in front, or nearly in front, of the play hole. If their opponents are not directly in the path of the play they can slide their men off to the side away from the play and go through to block off the secondary defense.

Against a standing defensive line, the offensive linemen should duck under the extended arms of their opponents to prevent being jabbed backward or held off by their opponents' stiff-arm charge.

In coming out of the line for interference a lineman should take his first step with the foot on the side toward which he is

LINE PLAY

7. Double Teaming,

8. or Two on One

9. High-Lowing

10. High-Lowing.

11. Opening Hole

12. Slicing Through

going to run. This foot should be brought back and about a foot to the side in the direction he is to go, so that he will be brought well back, and at the same time will make some progress with this first step. He shoves off with his other foot and the hand which is on the ground, and is helped make his turn by pressing upon his knee or thigh with the hand or forearm which rests upon the knee. Every lineman can learn to come out quickly and easily to either side, no matter which foot he has forward. The correct footwork is shown in the drawing.

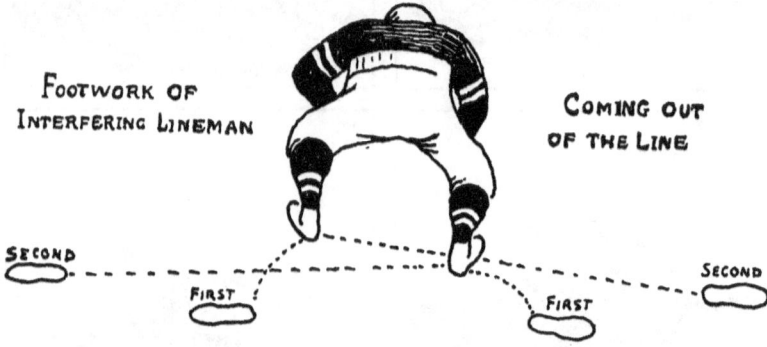

Fast runners are not so necessary in the interference but fast starters are the boys who are effective, because a quick start means more in a dash of ten yards than does speed in running, and ten yards is about as far as an interferer has to run in the average play. Plenty of practice should therefore be given the line interferers in starting from their positions in the line, and they should be taught not to point in the direction they are going, but always face straight ahead and give their opponents no intimation that they are going to pull out.

Linemen who are blocking in the line should be continually urged to go on down the field to block off the defensive backs after they have finished their line work, and not quit and look back to see how the play is progressing. Very often an opponent will dive low or hurl himself to the ground in such a way that the offensive linemen cannot get under him. In such cases the latter should go on over the prostrate opponent and not remain in the way of his own ball carrier, and he should not

LINE PLAY

look back to see what damage, if any, his opponent did to the play. All linemen should remember, as before stated, that a good interferer never looks back.

On defense the duties of ends, tackles, guards, and centers are so different that they are covered separately in the chapters dealing with individual positions. Some coaches prefer what is called a standing line defense in which all the men are on their feet with their hands ready to charge back their opponents, as shown in Drawing 4, their idea being that the five center men should drive their opponents back upon the initial charge, and, when they see where the play is going, work their way along the line to the spot attacked, without trying to break through. But the best defense for the whole line is to play low, with one or preferably both hands on the ground, as shown in Drawing 3. This is especially advisable for the three center men, who should charge holes instead of men.

Against an open or punt formation, or where the opponents have a large yardage to make, the standing line is preferable. For all linemen on defense a quick hard charge is necessary, and it is not necessary to watch the ball if the opponents are using a starting signal because the backs start as quickly as the ball does.

A common fault in defensive line play is that players, although they may assume a low stance, charge upward, and perhaps get through the line only to find themselves standing high and in no position to vary their course or to tackle the runner. They should charge low and keep low after the charge, and after breaking through they must always follow up the play.

HOW TO PLAY END

An end should be one of the headiest, quickest, and fastest men on the team. He should be what is commonly called "foxy" and not easily fooled. He need not necessarily be as large as the guards, center, and tackles, although the heavier an end is, provided he has the necessary speed and other qualifications, the more value he will be to his team. The tendency for several years has been to develop heavy ends. The game as now played requires of the end speed and greater skill in handling the ball, because of the open game and the fact that the handling of forward passes devolves upon him. These qualities are usually more highly developed in smaller players or those of medium weight, but the tackles and guards of defending teams now usually play so wide that their opposing tackles have to block the guards, and the end has to handle the tackle unaided. As the tackle is usually a strong and heavy man, the end whose duty it is to keep him from spoiling plays in his direction should be heavy enough to hold his own with him or his team will be severely handicapped when on the offensive. Where heavy, experienced material is scarce the lighter men are usually placed on the ends or back of the line, since weight is not so essential for those positions as for the five center men.

The end should be a low, sure tackler, able to avoid interference and to tackle in the open, and he should be quick and sure in falling on fumbled balls. He should also be able to handle forward passes without fumbling.

Offense

When his side has the ball, the end should stand on the line of scrimmage, with the outside foot forward and his inside hand or both hands upon the line, his back straight and tail lower than the shoulders, and his feet well apart to give him stability to withstand a charge or push from the side. An end should be careful not to be off-side, but he should always be up on a line with the ball and never back of the scrimmage line. He should face directly toward the opponent's goal line or at right angles to the line of scrimmage, and he should be close to his tackle unless the play formation calls for him to play wide. He should not allow the opposing tackle, by varying his position, to induce him to follow him. A foxy tackle will very likely move out wide or close in, to see if he can determine by the action of the opposing end where the play is coming. If the end follows him out, so as to be in a position to box him in on an end play, it will give the play away; therefore the end should line up in position with his eyes on the ball, and he should maintain that position until the ball is snapped. If the tackle plays too wide for the end to be able to box him in, the remedy is for the quarter, or whoever is directing the plays, to send plays inside of him. A few gains there will usually cause the tackle to close in, in order to defend his position.

Where the end has a wing back to aid him in handling the tackle he and this back should practice and develop team work so that each will know what part the other is to play in putting the opposing tackle out of the play.

The end should get into all regular plays which his quarter directs to the opposite side of the line outside of tackle. He should either leave his position with the snap of the ball and follow up the play to make the play safe, to watch out for fumbles and if one occurs to fall quickly on the ball or tackle the opponent who may secure it; or he should go through the line without blocking and cross over in front of the play to interfere for the runner in case he succeeds in getting past the opponent's line. On plays which are aimed at the opposite side of the line inside of tackle the end should always go through and block off one of the secondary defense. On plays which are aimed at his side of the line, the end should block the tackle. If the play is between center and guard, he should shoulder his opposing tackle out and go through and block off one of the backs, or interfere for the runner if the latter succeeds in getting through the line. Should the play be between the opposing guard and tackle on his side, or directed at the tackle, he should charge his man back and out, and stay with him until the play is stopped or the runner has passed. The end must block the tackle in when the play is outside of his position, or if the tackle is playing outside of him he may drive him back; but he must not let his opponent break through nor let himself be pushed back into the play. The tackle is a very dangerous man on plays of this kind, and unless he is pushed out of the way or blocked, the play will usually fail. As explained in the discussion of blocking and interfering, the end can make good use of his legs in preventing the tackle from getting to the runner, and he should not depend upon his shoulder alone.

On short forward passes, where he is supposed to be in a certain position to take the ball, the end should try to deceive his opponents by first blocking his man a moment, and then should run quickly to the spot where he is supposed to secure the pass. On long passes he should leave his position on the snap of the ball and get to the spot as quickly as he can. He must be able to catch the ball while running with his side or back to it, and should practice this until he is able to catch passes from any position. When the end is a decoy on a forward pass, he should play his part well. He should run hard and fast and try to make the opponents think he is the real receiver. The end should remember that good decoying is an important part of a forward-pass play.

On regular punts from scrimmage, kick-offs, trys for goal from fair catches, and punt-outs following touchbacks and safeties, the end should move out from his tackle from three to six yards, and go down the field the instant the ball is put into play. An end should be about the same distance out from his tackle no matter whether the signal calls for a punt, a pass, or a run, because if he plays closer in on some plays than he does on others the opponents will soon be able to diagnose the play from the position of the end. In going down the field under a kick he should not look back over his shoulder until he hears the thud of the kicker's foot as it meets the ball. He should use his hands on any opponent trying to block him and should keep well to the outside of the spot where the ball is going. He is the outside man, and if the player running back the ball gets around the end, he will make a good gain before the other tacklers can get to him, whereas even though the end is not able to tackle the man himself, if he forces him to the inside he will drive him toward other tacklers who will very likely down the runner before he has been able to make much progress. The end should be careful when nearing the man who has secured or is about to secure the ball, and should slow up so that he may not overrun the receiver nor allow him to side-step or dodge.

Defense

On defense the end should play about two to four yards from the tackle, the proper distance varying according to the system of defense his team is using. His duties will also vary on different teams for the same reason, and therefore I will only outline the duties that usually devolve upon the end under all systems of defense.

At the proper distance from the tackle, the end should assume a position similar to a sprinter on his mark, so as to be able to get a quick start. He should face slightly toward the opposing backs, watch the ball, and as soon as it is moved he should start almost straight forward, and not directly toward the backs unless he is playing a smashing type of end defense, in which case he should play in close and go in more sharply toward the backs. After he has his start, he can then see where the play is aimed and vary his course accordingly. If the play is coming toward his position he should meet it quickly and not hesitate or wait for the interference to get to him. He should keep well to the outside of the play, so that he will force the play inside of him toward his mates if he is not able to tackle the runner or stop the play himself. He should keep very close to the ground, and if he can avoid the interference or work his way through it and secure the runner, he should do so. If the interference is close and the runner well protected, he should hurl his body across the knees of the interferers, and the chances are that as they fall the runner will fall over them or will be forced to slow up to get around the pile and, unprotected, become an easy prey for the tackle or backs.

The main things for an end to remember are: first, that he must never wait for the play to come to him; and second, that he must meet it with his body close to the ground, and not standing up where the interferers can get at him with their shoulders.

If the play is aimed at the tackle or just inside, the end will be able to see it as he charges forward, and can throw himself inward and often tackle the runner from the side; but he should be careful not to do this unless he sees the ball in the player's arms, as the play may be a fake to draw him in.

If the play is aimed at the center, or at the other side of the line, the end should follow it up as fast as he can, being careful not to over-run any delayed passes or criss-cross plays. An excellent plan to adopt in following up plays from behind is to make it a point to always run over the place where the backs stood when starting, and then if any one of them is waiting to receive a delayed pass, the end will run over him. Having caught up with the play, the end should tackle the runner from behind if possible, and at all times he should be on the watch for fumbles. Under no circumstances should an end ever run around behind his own line to head off a play.

Most coaches play their ends on the line against the punt formation, except on fourth down when it is almost certain that a punt will be made. When playing on the line the ends rush to hurry the pass, block the punt, or tackle the runner in case an end run is attempted, leaving the defensive backs to block the opposing ends on punts or to intercept forward passes.

On fourth down, or whenever the end is sure the play will be a punt, he should as a rule play about five to seven yards back of the line and about the same distance out beyond his tackle, no matter whether the opposing end moves out or not. He will then be in a position to follow the opposing end down the field in case the ball is punted or a pass is made, or to rush up to head off the runner if it is a fake kick. He should not leave his position until he is sure what the play is to be. When he sees the ball punted, he should follow the end down the field on the inside of his opponent, bothering him all he can; and as the opponent slows up preparatory to tackling, the end should hurl his body at his knees or, if behind, clip him from the side and pin him to the ground.

If the opponents attempt a forward pass from the punt formation, the end, if he is playing back of the line of scrimmage, can usually size up the play before the pass is made. He should cover the halfback on his side of the center, leaving the defensive back on his side to cover the end.

The defense of the end against forward passes varies greatly under different coaching systems. Most coaches have their ends rush the passer at all times when the opponents are playing their regular close or running formation. When the opponents are in a loose formation with ends well out, as in a punt formation, some coaches depend upon the tackles to rush the passer and instruct the ends to delay the opposing ends in getting down the field and then to cover the "flat" territory—the territory near the scrimmage line and to either side of the offensive ends.

A heady end will vary his play somewhat on different downs and according to the distance the opponents have to go. On first downs the opposing field general will usually call for a play just inside or around the end, and therefore an end should look for a play of this kind and play almost as though he knew the play was coming in his direction. If the play is to the other side the end should follow up fast and try to catch the runner from behind and to prevent cut backs.

If an end is defending on the strong side of the opponent's formation he should play somewhat wider than he would if he were defending on the short side of an unbalanced formation.

On second and third downs, with only a short distance to gain, the defensive ends should play in closer and come in sharper, because a line smash is the play the opponents will most likely use when only a short gain is needed for first down.

Against an open or punt formation an end must not let an opponent flank him in such a way that he can be boxed in. When an opponent comes out wide and the end suspects that this opponent may be there to put him out of the play instead of to go down the field under a punt or to catch a pass, he should play a roving end and work back and forth along the scrimmage line, trying not to be in a position where the flanking opponent can get a good crack at him.

Whenever the ball goes out of bounds the defending end on that side of the field should be the last man to leave the side line when the ball is brought in, making sure that no opponent is left on the side line to receive a forward or lateral pass. After every play he should be careful that no opponent is left outside of his position, unnoticed, for a similar purpose.

The end should watch the ball closely and follow it swiftly at all times.

In the chapter on line play are drawings showing correct stances. Drawing 1 (page 73) shows a good position for an end to assume on both offense and defense. It is all right to have both hands on the ground, like a sprinter on his mark. If an end is playing a cautious game rather than the smashing style, it is perfectly all right for him either to have both hands on the ground or to adopt an upright stance. On defense the end's outside foot should be forward.

HOW TO PLAY TACKLE

The position of tackle is one of the most important on the team. Two good tackles are a valuable asset to any team, and in these positions the fastest and most experienced big men of the squad should be placed, since good, heavy, active tackles can do more damage to the opponent's offense than any other line players. Weight is not quite so essential for this position as for the position of guard, and speed is less important to the tackle than it is to the end, but a player who possesses both weight and speed, combined with a thorough knowledge of the game, should make an ideal tackle.

A tackle's duties are more varied than those of a guard, and when I have had to develop new tackles I have often found that an experienced guard could be made into a tackle, while it was much easier to make an inexperienced candidate into a guard than into a tackle. The position requires a very aggressive type of player and experience is a greater asset here than it is in the position of guard.

When his team has the ball, the tackle should stand as far forward as the rules allow, and close to the guard. He should maintain this position no matter how wide his opponent plays. He should have his outside foot forward (unless instructed differently by the coach), his inside hand or both hands upon the line, and his legs well under him and far enough apart to give him stability to withstand a side push. He should face squarely to the line of scrimmage, with his head up, his back straight, and no part of his body higher than his shoulders. He should keep his eyes on the ball unless his team is using a starting signal, in which case he might just as well watch his opponent. He should not by the least look or movement give his opponents an inkling as to where the play is to be directed, and in every play he should start the instant the ball is put in play or the starting signal given.

On regular plays directed to the opposite side of the line outside of tackle, he should leave his position to interfere on end runs. In starting for that purpose he should push off with the foot and hand which are on the line, and his first step should carry him back far enough so that he will not stumble over the legs of the other linemen. The correct steps for any lineman to take in coming out of the line are illustrated in the chapter headed "Line Play" (page 76).

If the play is to go inside of tackle on the other side, he should block his opposing tackle temporarily, and then go through to block off one of the defending backs; but if the play is directed between guard and center on his side he should let the end take care of the tackle and should himself help the guard with his man. On plays outside of the guard on his side of the line, whether end or tackle plays, the tackle should as a rule block the opposing guard, as this player usually plays so wide that his opponent is unable to box him in without help; and the guard may have to block the center. No rule can be laid down about this, since the plays may call for a lineman to block different opponents on different plays; but a fairly safe rule for any lineman to follow is to block the opponent to his right if the play is going to the left of his position, and to block the man on his left if the play is going to the right. The opposing tackle is usually beyond his blocking range, and will have to be taken care of by the end and the interference. Of course if the opposing guard and tackle are playing close in, the guard will then take care of his man alone, and the tackle will aid the end in putting the opposing tackle out of the play. The tackle will have to use his own judgment as to which of the opponents to block, being governed by their positions on the line; but the end and guard should always know which one of them he is to aid on a play.

When his team punts, the tackle need not block as long as the guards, and by a quick charge or a hard side push he should be able both to prevent his opponent from interfering with the punt and at the same time to get a quick start down the field to aid the ends in preventing the ball from being run back. The left tackle especially, provided the punter is right-footed, need hardly hesitate at all before going down the field, since his opponent, after being pushed outward, can very seldom get over in front of a right-footed punter. But the tackle should play safe and be sure to block long enough to avoid any danger of the kick being blocked.

On the defense the tackle should play about a yard and a half from his guard, and close to the line of scrimmage. He need not play quite so low as when on the offense, but it is well to have at least the inside hand upon the ground. He may face slightly toward the opposing backs, and should shift his position from time to time, in order to try to induce the opposing end to make some move which will give him a hint as to the direction of the play. He should note the formation of the opponents, and if there is more strength on one side of the ball than there is on the other, he should shift his position accordingly. Having gotten his position and his bearings, he should then watch the ball in order to get a quick charge, unless he knows the opponents are using a starting signal. In the latter case he had better watch the backs, because they start as quickly as the ball does, and there is no advantage in watching the ball. The instant the ball is snapped, the tackle should charge straight at the opposing end, who will very likely be in front of him, meeting him on the shoulders with arms extended and driving him back if possible. If a wing back or any other player is flanking him, or assisting the end in blocking him, he must either charge forward and by main strength and speed carry himself through before his opponents can converge upon him, or he must use his hands on one of them and brace himself to withstand the charge of the other. It is usually best to use the hands on the end rather than on the flanking opponent. He should at least keep the end from getting his body or shoulder against him, or from forcing him back. After charging the tackle will note the direction of the play. If it is directed outside of his position, he should push the end in and work his way out, in order to tackle the runner or break up the interference. If the play is aimed directly at his position or to the inside, he can either push the end back into it and jam it up, or he can shove the end to the side and dive into the play or tackle the runner. A tackle must guard the territory outside of his position: that is his primary duty. But he is also responsible for the territory between him and his guard, and therefore he must not play so wide that he can easily be blocked out.

Against an unbalanced line the tackle on the short side can play in much closer than he can when he is defending on the strong side of his opponent's formation, or when he is flanked by a back playing close to the line. On the weak side, with no one but the end to contend with, the tackle should play with his inside shoulder about opposite the outside shoulder of the offensive end, and in case the opponents' backs are shifted well over to the other or strong side, it may be advisable for the tackle to play exactly opposite, or perhaps a little inside, the end on the weak side.

If the play is going to the side away from the defensive tackle, he should follow the play up very fast, and under no circumstances should he pull back and run behind his own line to head off a play. When a tackle does this it shows that he is not charging, but is waiting to see where the play is going before making a move. A good tackle charges first and then varies his course according to the way the play is aiming. If he leaves his position to head off plays to the other side, then fakes, cut-backs, and reverse plays can be worked, the opponents faking at some other position and then coming through the hole he leaves open. If the tackle is always going through and following up plays going to the other side he will spoil fakes and cut-backs and he can often tackle the runner from behind when the latter is forced to slow up to change his course or to get around obstructing players. The tackle who follows up fast is also in a position to recover fumbles when they occur.

Tackles and ends often practice teamwork on the defense. This is a very good plan and can be used to great advantage by experienced players who understand each other, and have signals between themselves so that each will know what the other is going to do. For instance, the end might indicate to the tackle playing beside him that he is going to play in close and go in sharp and hard, in which case it would be well for the tackle to play more cautiously and not charge in recklessly, because the end, by going in fast and sharply, will break up the play, and the tackle must see that the runner does not run out wide. In a way the end is doing tackle duty while the tackle is doing end duty in such a case. Either the end or tackle might signal that the tackle was to charge in hard and recklessly and fast, in which case the end should play more of a cautious, waiting style. An end and tackle who can work together in this way, each varying his play in accordance with what the other is going to do, can raise havoc with their opponents, who will never know which style they have to meet.

If the smashing end style of defense is used the tackles

should play a little more cautiously than they need to when their ends are playing the cautious style.

A tackle should also use his head, and should know at all times the down and the distance to go. He can and should play wider when the opponents have a long distance to go to secure a first down, because in that case a wide or a trick play, or a pass, is much more likely to be used than is a power play into the line. When the opponents need but a short gain, the tackle should close in and play lower, and should charge harder and more toward the inside, because a line attack or a power play aimed directly at the tackle or a little to either side of him is very likely to follow.

Against a punt formation, or against an open formation of any kind, a tackle should play higher and can vary his play more. If a punt is likely, a tackle can usually break through better if he is on his feet than he can if he has one or both hands on the ground. He can also move about more. He should always go through on a punt or an open formation, and should try to block the kick, or if it is a pass to hurry the passer, unless as sometimes happens he is instructed by his coach to block his opponent to keep him from going down the field under the kick.

The defense of a tackle when a forward pass is expected varies under different systems of forward pass defense. Some coaches instruct their tackles to charge the ends and delay them in getting down the field and then to cover the flat territory against close or regular running formation where the ends are playing in close, and to rush the passer on punt formation or other open formations where the end is out wide. Other coaches instruct their tackles always to rush the passer when a pass is likely, leaving the ends to cover the flat territory; and still other good coaches have both ends and tackles rush the passer at all times.

The different methods of forward pass defense are discussed more fully in the chapter on defense.

At all times the tackle should follow the ball closely, and he should make it a practice to assist his backs to their feet after every play, giving them an encouraging slap on the back. Such acts on the part of players encourage and develop team spirit and morale.

When on the defense the great thing for a tackle to remem-

HOW TO PLAY TACKLE

ber is that he should be a veritable tiger, always fighting his way into the opponent's territory to get to the man with the ball, and fiercely overcoming all opposition with a determination which cannot be denied. A weakening on the part of the tackle invites attack, whereas a tackle who is hard to put out of a play forces the opponents to attack some more vulnerable position.

The correct positions for a tackle to assume, both upon offense and defense, are shown in the drawings illustrating the chapter on line play (page 73). The offensive stance is the same as that of a guard or end. Both the low and the standing defensive stances are shown.

HOW TO PLAY GUARD

The position of guard on a football team requires the least experience of any position on the team, for the reason that a guard has less territory to cover, and his duties are better defined and less varied than those of any other player. He has less opportunity for tackling, he seldom runs with the ball, and he can play a good game without being able to catch punts, pass, or kick. He has few chances to make sensational plays, and yet the backs on his team could gain little ground without his aid and protection.

The guard should be one of the heaviest men on the team. Strength—strength to withstand attack and break up the opponent's plays when they have the ball, and to make openings, protect the backs, and interfere when his own team is on the offensive—is the main qualification necessary to play his position.

While it is not necessary for the guard to be a particularly fast runner, he should by all means develop quickness in starting and a good leg drive, as these are absolutely essential to fast and effective charging. A quick start and fair speed are required in getting into the interference on plays around the opposite end, and no guard should be given a place on the team unless he is active and fast enough for this. Weight, speed, and aggressiveness combined make the ideal guard.

On offense a guard should stand with his feet on diagonally opposite corners of a square (or of a rectangle if he is particularly long-legged) with both feet and his whole body pointing straight ahead, at right angles to the line of scrimmage. The left guard generally has his left foot forward and the right guard his right, in order to enable them to get into the interference more readily on plays going around the opposite side. However, with practice it is just as easy to pull out of the line to the side on which a lineman has his forward foot. A guard should have the fingers of his inside or of both hands touching the ground, his head up, and his back straight and no part of it higher than his shoulders. The lower he can crouch the better, for when two men charge each other the great advantage lies with the one who keeps the lower and gets under his opponent.

He should keep his head up, so that he can watch the ball and the opposing backs as well as his immediate opponents.

The most successful position for a guard, and the one most generally adopted in playing on the defensive, has been explained in the chapter on line play: he stands, resting *both* hands on the ground, at a distance of a yard or a little more from his center. If the formation of the opponents is regular, the guard's position should be a little outside of his opponent, but he should shift to the right or left, as the case may be, if he sees the opponents have a one-sided formation.

A guard's duties on defense are chiefly to protect his position, and the space between him and his tackle, from plays aimed at those places, and he may be able to aid in stopping plays aimed at the center by pushing his opponent into them.

When the opponents have the ball, the guard should note the formation of the opposing backs, and then keep his eyes on the ball unless a starting signal is being used, when he should watch the opposing backs for the start. He will be able to see the position of his direct opponent while watching the ball or the backs. If the opponents are slow in forming, he can often determine by looking at the backs on which side of the line the play will come, since very often some back will give the play away by his actions. *A guard should always charge the instant the ball is snapped.* This rule is invariable whether on offense or defense, except when his side is kicking; because the man who "gets the charge" on his opponent has a great advantage. If the guard sees the play coming at him he may either throw his opponent to one side and himself drop in front of the play at the knees of the oncoming men, or he may charge his opponent back directly in front of the play. If the play is not coming into his territory he should charge through, not allowing his opponent to block him, and if he cannot get the man with the ball, he will at least be able, with shoulders and body, to cut off several players who are interfering. The guard should try to break through the opponent's line on defense and he should not engage in a personal encounter with his opponent. What he should aim to do is to avoid his opponents and get through them, and therefore it is best to charge through openings between opponents, rather than to charge men. In breaking through, a good method is first to shoot the arms between the opponents while charging forward, and force the opponents apart with the arms. Another method is to turn the shoulders so that they will be at right angles to the ground and knife through, as shown in Drawing 12 illustrating the chapter on line play (page 75). While playing this way he must watch the ball, and make sure that no criss-cross or "split play" or fake comes through his position. If the play goes around the opposite side, he should follow around at top speed, and by so doing he can often catch the runner from behind and can also prevent cutbacks.

The guard should follow the ball always. By charging through fast, with his eyes always on the ball, he can prevent the opposing backs from getting off quick kicks and forward passes. When the opposing team kicks, he must charge through fast and attempt to block the kick by jumping in the air and throwing up his arms at the proper time. He must also be keen to see and to frustrate a fake kick through the line.

While as a general rule a defensive guard should play low and charge through the line, there are times when it is advisable for him to play on his feet and not attempt to charge through. When the opponents have a long distance to go for a first down it is not likely that they will attempt a line buck which would stand little chance of gaining the desired distance, and therefore they will most likely try a wide play or a forward pass. The guards can be of more value, in such a case, by playing high, first seeing that no attack is made into the line and then pulling out to head off an end run or receding to help defend against a forward pass. This style of guard defense is also advisable against spread plays.

On the offense the guard should play close to the center and it is not necessary that he should have both hands on the ground, although this is the position sometimes assumed. If only one hand is on the ground it should be the hand nearest the center, and the opposite elbow should rest upon the knee.

A guard must never allow his opponent to charge through and interfere with the plays and he should never allow his opponent to charge him back. He should, whenever possible, "get the charge" on his opponent. In making holes for plays, the guard need not, and often cannot, get his opponent entirely out of the path of the play; but he should get his own body on the side of his opponent to which the play is coming, and charge him backward and away from the play. If he is unable to move his opponent, but gets under him and gets the charge on him, the backs, with their momentum when they hit the line, will force the opponent backward, and the play will gain ground. A "foxy" guard can often mislead his opponent as to where the play will come, so that the opponent will almost get himself out of the way by charging in the wrong direction. A guard should "size up" his opponent so that he can take advantage of his weaknesses and can get him out of the way more easily. If he stands high, the guard may charge under him and up, so that when the backs strike the line he will go over backwards. If he stands so low that it is impossible to get under him, his head can be pushed to the ground so that he cannot see or get at the play.

One of the chief points of a guard's usefulness to his team is in leading or getting into the interference on plays going around the opposite end or tackle. He should start the instant the ball is snapped. He should run with knees high and should ward off tacklers with shoulders and body.

A guard should always be standing over the back who has been tackled, ready to help him up and give him an encouraging word. The backs are usually smaller men, and they get some severe jolts from the opposing tacklers. The aid and protection of the big linemen help them materially.

Always, on offensive or defensive, a guard should "line up" or get into position as soon as the ball is in place. After a play, particularly a line play, has passed the line and the guard has charged his opponent out of the way, he should continue with the runner, blocking off the secondary defense and warding off tacklers.

When a punt is planned, a guard's first duty is to prevent anyone coming through his territory and blocking the kick. He need not block longer than to allow the punter to get the kick off safely, then he should get down the field at top speed and tackle the man who catches the punt, or be ready to get the ball if it is fumbled. If the guard finds that no back attempts to block the punt by coming through his territory, often by making an extra-quick start and hard charge, he can get his opponent off his feet, or tangled up at one side, and can himself get away down the field almost as quickly as the ends; and when he once gets started he usually has a clear field, for very seldom are men coached to block him as they do the ends. Getting down the field on kicks in this way will give the guard more chances to make open-field tackles than he is liable to get at any other time during the game, except on kick-offs, where he has the same opportunity.

When his team is going to make a forward pass the guard will be detailed either to block in the line or to pull back and protect the passer, and in either case he should quickly follow up the pass after blocking, so as to prevent any run-back in case the pass should be intercepted.

The guard, besides having strength, must have confidence in himself and should never at any stage of the game or under any circumstances show signs of weakening. His opponent will very likely play his hardest and roughest and do considerable bluffing early in the game, in order to test the guard's nerve, strength, and mettle; and if he succeeds in bulldozing or getting the better of him, it will give the opponent encouragement and confidence which will cause him to play harder as the game progresses. On the other hand, a good stiff opposition will tend to discourage his opponent and cause him to let up in his efforts.

HOW TO PLAY CENTER

The center should be a heavy man and at the same time should be an active player with a good head, steady, and not easily rattled. Many good centers have been comparatively small men, but weight, combined with activity, experience, and brains, enables a player in this position to do the best work both on the offense and defense.

The center occupies a very conspicuous position, because he handles the ball in all plays when his team is on the offense, and the ball and the player in whose possession it is are always in the spectator's eye.

The systems of defense generally used often call for the center to play behind the line instead of in the line, and in that case he is doing backfield defensive duty. If the system of defense his team uses calls for him to be in and out of the line under different situations, he must use good judgment in knowing which particular style of defense to play, and a center playing this variable style of defense must be an experienced man, an excellent tackler, and a heady all-round player. If he always plays in the line, a less experienced player and one not so active will fill the bill.

On offense the center should stand with his feet well apart, one foot somewhat farther advanced than the other, and both feet well under him so that he will rest little or no weight on the ball. His tail should be low and his back straight. A good stance for center is shown in the drawings illustrating this chapter. If he uses the end-over-end pass he should grasp the ball somewhat back of its center and on its sides. If using the spiral pass, he should have one hand more under the ball and the other farther forward and toward the top of the ball. Either method of passing the ball to the backs is good form. The end-over-end pass is the easiest to learn and the easiest for the backs to handle, and repeated timing with a stop watch has shown that the simple end-over-end pass is just as fast in getting the ball to the punter as is the more intricate spiral. The spiral pass from center has absolutely no advantages over the end-over-end method as far as I have been able to determine, and I never encourage or teach it; but, as stated above, either method is good.

Offensive Center, End-Over-End Pass — Same, Spiral Pass

The center, above all things else, must be a steady and accurate passer. If the backs are worried about how the ball is coming to them they become nervous and cannot get off to a quick start, and disastrous fumbles occur. When a quarterback is used to handle the ball, the pass is almost a hand-to-hand pass and is not hard to make; but when the team is using the direct-pass method, with the ball going directly to the runner, accurate and steady passing is doubly essential and such passing requires plenty of practice. The pass should go to the runner waist high, and if he is running to either side the ball should be fed to him in such a way that the back can take it at full speed and not have to slow up or wait for the ball before starting. In all direct passing (except long passes to a punter or passer, when speed in getting off the punt or pass is necessary), the passes need not be and should not be swift. Easy, lob passes are much easier for the backs to handle and they need not slow up the runner, provided the ball is floated well in front of him so that he can take it at full speed.

The center's first duty is to get the ball accurately to the runner, but he can, with practice, learn to pass and charge almost with one movement, his arms and the ball moving backward while his body is moving forward to block an opponent. Where the indirect, quarterback pass is used the center need not look at the quarter; but where the ball is being passed directly to the runner he should be looking at the runner while passing.

After passing, the center should endeavor to get his head or body between his opponent and the play, and charge him away from the path of the runner. If it is a wide play he should go on through after blocking and try to get ahead of the runner as an interferer, blocking off the secondary defense. If the play is coming through the line at or near his position, he should of course charge straight into his opponent, carrying him back and out of the path of the runner.

A very important thing for the center to remember is that he should always follow the ball closely, and be ready to take it from the runner as soon as the latter is stopped. This is necessary because the runner should not leave the ball upon the ground unprotected, and the center should be there to receive it in order to enable the man who has carried it to get back quickly into his position. A team cannot play a fast game if the center is slow in following the ball and getting into position for the next play. The opposing center may slyly push the ball back a few inches after each down unless he is watched closely and the ball is well protected, and this may prove costly to the offensive team in cases where the ball is lost on downs by a narrow margin.

In passing the ball back for a punt, the center should practice the long pass until he can get the ball back swiftly and accurately without first moving or raising the ball from the ground. On these passes he should watch the man to whom the pass is made, and take a great deal of care in getting the ball to him cleanly. If the punter has to reach high or low or to the side to get the ball, it throws him out of position and interferes with his punting. It also makes the liability of a fumble greater. Great care should be taken not to pass the ball too high, because it may go over the punter's head with disastrous results. The pass had better be too low than too high. After passing the ball to the punter, the center should block his man long enough to prevent him from getting through in time to block the kick, and then go down the field as fast as possible.

The method of playing center on defense differs according to the system of defense the team is using. Some centers are coached to play rather high and about a yard back from the scrimmage line. In this position they watch the direction of the play and head it off wherever it is aimed, running around behind their own line if the play starts around the end or outside of tackle. By playing in this way the center can get into every play, and make the defense stronger in stopping plays in any direction except toward the center of the line. In order to play this method of defense properly, the center has to watch the backs and start the instant they start. If he sees the play start for his position he goes into it and meets it low. The weak point in this system of playing defensive center is that it renders the center of the line more vulnerable to regular line-bucking plays, and especially to fake plays which start for some other point to draw the center away and then shoot through the unguarded position.

When his team is using a six-man-line defense the center plays back and backs up the line the same as a defensive back. His duties under this system are explained in the chapter dealing with the backfield.

If the center plays in the line on defense he should play low, with both hands on the ground, watching the ball and charging through the line either to the right or left of his opponent, varying this by occasionally charging his opponent back upon the quarter. By playing in this way the player gets a quicker charge, because he is in a better charging position, is watching the ball instead of the backs, and never hesitates to see where the play is going before the charge is made. He is also better able to guard the center of the line from fake as well as from regular line plays, because the player is always going through and will meet those methods of attack.

The center should usually move over if the opponents have more strength on one side of the ball than on the other, and go through on that side. If he always goes through, or charges his man back, the center will not only meet any play coming at him, but should the play be going around either end he will also block off the line interference, and by following up the play he can very often tackle the runner from behind. If he happens to charge through one side of center, and the play comes through on the other side, of course there will be an opening there; but a good defensive back is usually backing up the center, and the opening in the line will enable the defensive back to meet the play before it reaches the hole, or at least before the line is crossed.

If his team is always using a seven-man-line defense, the

center should play high and should not attempt to go through when the opponents have a large yardage to make. In that case he first makes sure that the play is not coming through his position, and then backs out to cover territory, if a pass is being attempted, or to head off the play if it is an end run. This is the way he should also play against a spread, or any other open formation.

The center should always get to the ball quickly when on the defense, as well as when his own side has the ball, not only because any good defensive player always follows the ball closely, but also because if he is not on the spot when the opposing center takes the ball from the runner the latter will often move it ahead in placing it in position for the next scrimmage, thus gaining a few inches on every play. The defensive center should not only prevent this, but should also watch the opponent who is bringing in the ball from out of bounds, to see that he does not gain any ground by the operation but brings it in at right angles to the spot where it went out.

When the other side forms for a kick the center should play high, and should either go through to block the kick and hurry the kicker, or, by prearrangement, make a hole for some other player to go through. But if he is playing out of the line he should block the first man through the line if the play is a kick.

HOW TO PLAY THE BACKFIELD

The duties of all players in the backfield are so nearly alike that all of the backfield positions will be covered under the above head.

The qualifications necessary for a backfield player are speed, cleverness in handling the ball, and ability to tackle and interfere. A back need not necessarily be a heavyweight, but he must be of rugged type and able to stand hard collisions and rough handling, because the players carrying the ball are always in the center of the scrimmage and many times during a game must stand the shock of being tackled and thrown to the ground.

Somewhat different types of players are required for the different positions back of the line. One of them should be a good field general and leader, to direct his team and call the signals. At least one of the backfield men should have plenty of weight and should be an unusually strong runner. Such a back is necessary to do the line-smashing work, and he is of great value in backing up the line on defense. There should be at least one back, preferably two, who are fast and clever open-field runners, for use in the wide plays which require speed and elusiveness. At least one of the backs must be a good punter and there must be one or two good forward passers among the four. If one back combines ability to run with the ball, kick, and forward pass, he is called a triple-threat man and is a very valuable player to any team. The open-field runners should be well drilled in dodging and eluding tacklers and in the use of the stiff-arm, and all of the backs should be players who can hang onto the ball and not fumble when tackled and thrown. A fumbling back is a detriment to any team. If only three good ball-carrying backs are available, one man can be used in the backfield who does not have the ability to tote the ball, but who is a good interferer.

All the backfield men should be well drilled in all the rudiments of the game. They should all be quick to think and to act, and above all they should be fearless and able to stand punishment.

Small, nifty, dodging and side-stepping backs often get away for long and spectacular runs against weak opposition and may look to be better than the heavier and less clever fellows under those conditions, but against strong opposition, when the going is tough, the clever little backs are likely to lose as much ground as they gain. The big, hard-running backs who depend upon their weight and power rather than upon cleverness in avoiding tacklers will generally prove to be much more consistent, though less spectacular, ground gainers, and the latter type of ball-carriers seldom lose any ground. The majority of football fans know very little about the finer points of football. They like to see open play and they will show great enthusiasm when they see a back dodge and sidestep and perhaps reverse his field and elude several tacklers, even though the runner is eventually tackled for no gain or for a loss; and they wonder why the coach does not use a back showing so much cleverness. A coach picks his backs for their ability to run toward the opponent's goal and not for their cleverness in running parallel to it, and he should not let enthusiasm of the fans, or newspaper comment, influence him in the selection of his players.

His business is to select not those men who show up the best against the smaller teams, but those who come through when the going is the toughest. The heavier back will also prove to be the better man in the interference, a better man to follow interference, and a better man to aid in handling the tackle when the back is placed on the wing. The chances are that he will also prove a much better man on defense; and, being heavier and more powerful, he is less susceptible to injuries than is the lighter man.

The Field General

One of the backfield men is usually selected as field general and the caller of the signals. This important duty in former days was generally assigned to the quarterback, but any backfield player can act in that capacity—in fact a line player can do it if he is found to have better judgment and qualities of leadership than any backfield man. Whether lineman or back, the field general should be the headiest, peppiest, scrappiest, and most enthusiastic man on the team, and he should have the entire confidence of his team-mates. He is the general directing the attack, and he should know what to do under all the varying conditions which may confront him. He should be supreme and should brook no interference from his team-mates, with the exception of his captain under whom he works.

If the huddle system is not used, the field general should give his signals in such a tone of voice and in such a manner that they will be easily heard and understood. It is quite generally recognized that a team will execute its plays in about the same spirit in which the orders are given. If the field general gives his signals in a slow and indecisive and deliberate manner, the team will execute the plays in about the same listless way, whereas if he calls out the signals in a snappy, decisive, and gingery way, his team reflects that spirit in executing his orders.

The field general should never for a moment show the least sign of lack of confidence in his team to gain ground. If the strongest plays do not gain at the start of the game, it would be fatal for him to let his team see any sign of hesitancy or discouragement. Rather should he try, by every possible means, to put more fight into his men and keep plugging away and urging the players to greater efforts. Such a leader will very likely get his team to put on more steam, and gradually the plays will begin working and a victory be gained which might easily have been turned into a rout for his team if the leader had allowed himself to become discouraged when his pet plays were broken up early in the game. Discouragement is another name for quitting, and there should be no such word in the vocabulary of a football player.

The Line Plunger

One man in the backfield should be a line-bucking specialist. This player needs weight and power more than do the end-running backs. He should be a crashing type of player who can force his way through the strongest opposition, and he should be able to keep his feet and hang on to the ball. If he is hitting into the line from a position rather close up, say from within four yards, he should always go where the signal calls for the hole to be made, and not look for any other opening. If an interferer precedes him in a tandem attack he should always hit the line directly back of the front man in the tandem, so that their combined power and momentum will force a gain even if no hole is made or the opponents are not taken out of the play.

If he hesitates in order to look for an opening he has no power, and his usefulness as a line-crashing back is gone. If a back is hitting into the line from a position well back, say five or more yards, he has time to vary his course to hit into an opening at either side of the spot at which the play is aimed without slackening his speed and without hesitating at the start; but the close-up line-plunger should never attempt such a variation.

A line-plunging back should hang on to the ball with both hands until he is past the line of scrimmage, so that it may be less easily torn or knocked from his grasp. He should run low and with his speed increasing at every step, and when he meets opposition he should take short digging steps with his feet well apart so that he cannot easily be deflected to the side or lose his balance. If there is no hole, and especially if only a short yardage is needed and the opposing line is playing very low, he should dive over his opponents, but ordinarily he should step high so as not to stumble over the opposition. A good illustration of about how a line-plunging back should run at an opposing line would be to go at it in about the way he would try to crash through a thick and tangled hedge. If he hits in an upright position he not only presents a larger surface to the obstruction, but he is likely to fall backward if he fails, whereas if he runs low and hits with his head and shoulders he meets less opposition and will seldom or never lose any ground.

The Running Backs

Every backfield should contain at least one and preferably two good, speedy, clever open-field runners, for use in off-tackle plays and end runs. Weight is not as essential for such work as it is for line plunging, but, as has been stated, weight is a valuable asset in open-field or end running if it is accompanied by speed.

The open-field runner should not only be speedy but he should also be clever in dodging and side-stepping and stiff-arming opponents who get in his path. He should never give ground or run back in trying to get around an opponent, and he should always take full advantage of his interference as long as it can possibly be of any use to him. The back who runs wild and does not follow his interference should not be tolerated on any team. When his interference has enabled him to get beyond the scrimmage line he can make use of his dodging and elusive running to good advantage. An end-running back should carry the ball under his right arm if running to the right, and under the left if running to the left, so that he will have his free arm to use on the side where the most opposition is likely to be encountered. The correct way of placing and carrying the ball is shown in the drawings illustrating tackling and blocking. When tackled the ball carrier should get both hands on the ball so as not to lose his hold on it when falling.

If another back is running in a position to receive a lateral pass, a back can carry the ball in front of him in both hands to threaten or actually to make a lateral pass. Or if he gets out in the open with only one opponent to dodge, he can bring the ball out in front of him with both hands so that he can place it quickly under either arm when he decides on which side of the tackler he is going to pass, thus freeing for his defense the arm on the side next his opponent. But as a general rule it is not good form to use this rugby method of carrying the ball in our American game.

We have now covered the duties of backs when carrying the ball, but that is only a part of the offensive duties of good backfield men. They should be good at interfering for the runner, and should work just as hard at this as they do when they themselves are carrying the ball, because ground gaining depends upon team work, good interference, and good blocking fully as much as it does on the hard and clever running of the

1. FRONT VIEW. BACKFIELD OFFENSIVE

2. SAME, SIDE VIEW

man with the ball. No man should hope to be placed in the backfield if he is not a good interferer, or if he is inclined to loaf when a team-mate is carrying the ball, only putting forth his best efforts when he himself has a chance to be in the limelight as the ball toter.

Most teams use a backfield man as a wing back to help the end in handling the defensive tackle, and here again the heavier back has an advantage. In working on the tackle the end and back either double-team him and carry him away from the path of the play, or they work the high-low on him, the end hitting the tackle with his body on the inside and low, and the half driving at him rather high with the shoulder block and dumping him over the end. If the tackle is to be blocked out for a play inside of his position the back hits him low and the end hits him high. A wing back, being outside of the tackle, has a great chance to do the latter a lot of damage, and a back who is efficient in this work is of great value.

Offensive play of the backfield has now been covered, with the exception of punting, forward passing, catching passes, and so on, which departments of play were discussed in previous chapters and need not be reconsidered here. But the explanation of the proper offensive stance and the correct method of starting still has to be given.

If a team is using a shifting-backfield style of offense, the backs should be on their feet, which are placed well apart, with hands on knees. In this position they are better able to change their positions quickly by means of steps or by a jump, and after shifting they usually maintain the same standing stance. Such stances are shown in Drawings 3 and 4.

When a team is not using the backfield shift the correct standard stance of offensive backs is shown in Drawings 1 and 2. The feet are well apart and one may be slightly in advance of the other, although it is just as well to have them even. Some weight is resting on one hand on the ground and the other hand either rests on the knee or is held well back. In this position the backs should watch the ball and should be sure not to lean or point in the direction they are going. Defensive players are quick to note any sign the offensive backs may inadvertently give by means of a glance or a slight change of position which may indicate where the play is going.

When starting straight forward, or at an angle, the backs get away in much the same manner as does a sprinter, but when starting to the side a back should make his first step with the foot on the side toward which he is to run. When he raises that foot he must instantly move in that direction because his center of gravity is far to that side of the foot supporting his weight. If he starts off by taking a step with his far foot he first has to shift his weight to the other side by leaning that way. He can also start directly parallel to the scrimmage line much easier by stepping first with the foot on the side toward which he is going than he can by taking the first step with the opposite foot, because the latter method is inclined to make his first step carry him somewhat forward and not directly to the side.

Backfield Defense

The backfield players should be chosen as much for their defensive ability as for their ball-carrying and interfering effectiveness. The different systems of backfield defense are discussed in the chapter on defense, but under any system of defense many of the duties of the backs are the same. All of the backfield men must be expert tacklers, and they should all be quick to size up every situation and to know by the down, the distance to gain, and the position on the field about what type of play the opponents are likely to use. They should all study generalship and field strategy just as much as does the man who is their own field general, so that they can outguess the offensive

team and be prepared to meet the play which in a given situation a good field general would be likely to use. Any system of backfield defense should vary under different conditions.

The correct stance of defensive backfield players is shown in Drawings 3 and 4. They should be on their feet, their feet well apart, and should lean forward with hands on knees. They should watch the opposing backfield very closely, so that they can move the instant the offensive team starts.

The man backing up the line, or the two men if a box defense or a six-man-line is used, should stand from two to five yards behind the defensive linemen, varying the distance in accordance with the down and distance to go. It stands to reason that players backing up the line should play closer up when expecting a line attack, and farther back when an open play is more likely to be tried. If the opponents have a large yardage to make, the defense to line plays may be weakened in order that the players may be in a better position to stop wide plays or forward passes. Although a line play might be used in such a case, the chances are that it can be stopped before the desired distance can be gained. When a line attack is likely to be used, a man backing up the line should be no farther back of his line than the offensive player who usually is used for line-bucking purposes. If he is farther back, assuming that both start at the same time, the defensive back cannot meet the ball-carrier until he has crossed the scrimmage line and made some gain, whereas he should be near enough to meet a line-plunger on the line, or a little back of it if a hole is opened in his forward wall.

A player backing up the line is the most important defensive man on his team, because he gets into every play and heads off the runner wherever he goes. The primary duty of a defensive line is to break up the plays, and of course to tackle the runner if they can; but if they break up the plays and are never pushed back a man backing up the line can usually tackle the runner.

The backs should watch the heads of the offensive backfield, because their heads are the first part of their bodies to move and so to indicate the direction of the play. When the man backing up the line sees where the ball carrier is heading for, he should not hesitate, but instantly start to meet the runner on the scrimmage line, whether the runner is coming straight into the line or going to either side. If he sees the ball carrier running back, he realizes quickly a pass is coming, and he either backs up or covers his assignment, according to whether his team is using a zone or a man-to-man defense for passes. If a punt is the logical play, a player backing up the line may sometimes come up on the line to try to block the punt, but usually he drops back a little farther and blocks off the first opponent coming through the line to run down under the punt.

Good, hard, sharp tackling by players backing up a line does much to slow down and discourage the opposing backs, and line-plungers who come through the line alone should be easy prey for a good defensive back. If a player precedes the ball-carrier on line plays, then the man backing up the line should stop the front man and not allow himself to be blocked out of the play. A man backing up a line should never get up so close to his line that he will be cut off from plays to either flank by having his own linemen shoved back in his way, and he should never rush in blindly. He should first see where the play is aiming for, and then without hesitation aim to meet the play on the line. The biggest and best tackler among the backs is usually selected for this most important defensive position.

The position of the two backs who are stationed farther back from the line and on either side is not so favorable for stopping running plays, and these men are primarily responsible for stopping forward passes. Their distance from the line varies according to the type of defense used, and also with different conditions of play. In a box defense they should play farther back than they would in a diamond defense, and not quite as wide, because in the box defense there is no safety man and the two rear backs must be far enough to the rear to enable them to get back quickly if a surprise punt is played, and also to cover deep pass receivers. They can afford to play farther back because there are two backs close up, whereas in the diamond defense there is only one.

In a diamond defense the two halfbacks play about seven to ten yards back and a little outside their ends. If the ends are playing a reckless, smashing game the halfbacks should play a little wider than is necessary if their ends are playing farther out and playing a cautious game. In the first case more runners are likely to get around the defensive ends and the halfbacks must be in a position to come up on the outside and stop wide plays, whereas ends playing a cautious game will seldom allow a runner to get around them. In a box defense the backs farthest in the rear need not play so wide, because two men backing up the line can stop wide plays more easily than can only one back playing close up.

No matter which system is used, the rear backs should come up fast when they see that a running play is being made, and head it off wherever it is going. Backs playing in these positions too often think that they are back there simply to defend against passes and punts, and they are slow to come up to help in stopping regular running plays. These defensive backs should be able to prevent runs around the end, and by coming up fast they will prevent many long runs by backs who have succeeded in getting through the line.

If the field is muddy and the ball is slippery the rear backs can play much closer to the line, because forward passes, especially long ones, are hard to execute with a slippery ball. They can also play closer if the wind is against the passer or punter. Their duties when the opponents are passing will be governed by the system of pass defense being used. They will have certain men to cover if playing a man-to-man defense, while in a zone defense they will have certain defined territory to cover; but whatever the system used they should watch the ball as well as the man they are covering and play the ball after the pass is made. They should be careful not to let a pass receiver get by them and they should use good judgment in knowing when to bat the ball down and when to try to intercept it, only doing the latter when there is absolutely no chance for an opponent to get his hands on the ball and never attempting to intercept on fourth down unless they have a clear field ahead of them.

When the opponents punt, the rear backs who are not back to receive the kick should block the opposing ends from getting down the field. In doing this it is best not to try to block them near the line, but instead to follow them down and do the blocking just as the ends slow up preparatory to tackling. If the ends are going straight at the punt receiver they should be blocked in, but it is usual for ends to keep well to the outside and in that case they can be blocked to the outside more easily, thus allowing the runner to advance straight up the field instead of trying to circle the ends.

FOOTBALL PRACTICE

A playing knowledge of the game of football, a formidable defense, and splendid team work can only be secured as the result of weeks and months of regular practice. It is important then that this practice be intelligently conducted, and it is hoped that the following discussion of methods of teaching rudiments, and suggestions as to how and what to practice, will materially aid both coaches and players in obtaining the best results with as little waste of time and effort as possible.

When the players first appear for practice it is a good plan to have them jog a couple of times around the field the first thing they do in order to get them limbered up and ready to go. After that they should busy themselves at some specialty work while the squad is gathering. The ends should be catching passes, the punters punting with a center passing the ball, other backs catching the punts, place-kickers practicing goal kicking, the kick-off men at work, and the guards and tackles practicing starts and the correct steps in coming out of the line. Everyone should be busy at something on which he needs practice, and there should be plenty of balls for the players' use.

When about all the men are present it is a good plan early in the season to start the systematized work with a setting-up drill for about ten or fifteen minutes. In this work body bending and twisting movements should be stressed, part of the work being given with the players standing and part of it with them on their stomachs and backs. This should be followed by practice in the rudiments of the game; in the early season the squad should be given much practice in falling on the ball, picking up a loose ball, tackling, blocking, charging, and so on.

After the first few days of the season the practice of rudiments usually becomes monotonous, hard, and uninteresting work for the players—so much so that some players will come to practice late, in order to miss this daily grind and be fresh for the scrimmage practice which usually follows it.

The practice of these fundamentals is absolutely necessary if the players are to become proficient in all departments of the game, and therefore plans should be devised and followed which will make practice preliminary to the scrimmage as interesting as possible, and not simply cold-blooded routine work. After the season is well started the setting-up work and the practice of the rudiments can better be conducted at the end of the practice period instead of at the start. Darkness or poor light which shortens the practice period late in the season does not interfere with this work as much as it does with signal drill and scrimmage.

The practice of the rudiments—falling on the ball, tackling, blocking, etc.—can be shortened and perhaps dispensed with altogether after the middle of the season, but it should not be neglected in the early season. My observation has been that most high-school coaches neglect such practice too much, although the school boys need rudimentary work much more than do the more advanced college players. Such practice is valuable not only for the purpose of teaching the men the proper way of doing the things good players have to do, but also for conditioning and hardening the players and getting them accustomed to the hard bumps they will receive by coming into contact with the ground and with other players.

Side tackling, in which the shoulder is not used, can best be practiced by the players tackling each other, alternating in tackling and being tackled. In this practice the player to be tackled stands about two yards from the tackler facing at right angles to him and the tackler takes one step with the foot on the side on which the runner is being tackled. Driving off that foot, the tackler shoots his body across in front of the standing player and hooks his outside arm well around the knees. Correct form is taught in this way, the tackler and the player being tackled facing both to the right and to the left so that the players learn to tackle equally well on either side. When they have mastered the correct form the men being tackled can jog past the tacklers so that practice is had under more difficult conditions.

In practicing the straight-on shoulder tackle the dummy should be used because it does just as well and practice in tackling each other in this way is too rough work to be indulged in to any great extent.

In all this tackling practice there is no need of running hard, or tackling roughly, since the development of correct form is the important consideration.

A good way to practice open-field tackling, and at the same time develop the backs in the use of the stiff-arm and in carrying the ball in the open field, is to place a lineman on every other five-yard line from one goal to the other or half the length of the field. Then start the backs with the ball, one at a time, from one goal line, and let them endeavor to run through these tacklers without being tackled any oftener than they can help. The linemen should be instructed not to cross the line in front of them, although they can move across the field from side to side in order to keep in front of the runner. While this is a very valuable practice, it is hard and rough work, especially for the backs, and should not be tried oftener than about one day of the week. It can be varied by having the backs and linemen change positions, as the backs need practice in open field tackling and it will benefit the linemen to practice running with the ball.

The clipping, or rolling, or Indian block should be practiced on the dummy about as much as is tackling. To get the correct form the players can also go through this method of blocking without hitting anything at all.

Charging practice should be employed freely by using the charging sled, by charging out on the ground, in which the players take one or two steps and then shoot their bodies forward on the ground, and by charging each other. Good practice is gained by lining the men up opposite each other and at a given signal having them try to shove each other back, using only their shoulders. The players will soon find that the one who charges the lowest in this work has the advantage. It teaches them to charge and block low, and to try to get under their opponents.

In nearly everything a player does he uses a good, hard leg drive. In tackling he crouches low and drives at the runner by a strong leg drive. In falling on the ball he shoots his body forward in the same way. In blocking and interfering he gets in a hard leg drive when he hits his man. A good leg drive is necessary in charging through the line on the defense and in charging men out of the way on the offense. Since the leg drive is so important, it should be thoroughly developed, and nothing develops it better than work on the charging sled, charging forward on the ground, or charging against other players.

When practicing catching punts, the backs should not only catch the ball, but they should place it quickly under the arm and start down the field. Whenever they fumble or miss the catch, they should fall upon the ball. They will regard this as a penalty, and will be more careful to catch the ball than they would be if they did not have to fall on it when they fumbled.

At least once or twice a week there should be practice in running down on punts. The backs stationed to receive the punts should work in pairs, one catching and the other interfering for him. The linemen should be spread out on a line about five yards back of the ball, so as to give them a clear vision of it, and to enable the punter to kick far enough to give the backs a chance to catch the ball before the tacklers are upon them. The linemen should be numbered off so that not more than four or five will have the same number and go down at one time. In this practice the punter should direct the tacklers by calling out "right," "left," or "short" as soon as he notes the direction and distance he has punted.

In practicing the rudiments the squad is usually divided, the backs being in one group and the linemen in the other. The backs may then be practicing passing or punting and catching while the linemen are charging, or one bunch can be using the tackling dummy while the other is falling on the ball, thus keeping all the players systematically busy at something.

System in practice is a great help, and is necessary where only a short time can be devoted each day to practice. An hour and a half is long enough for any squad to practice, provided the players are all on hand at the same time and the practice is so systematized that no time is wasted. The backs can usually hustle on their suits and get sufficient practice in punting and catching punts while the rest of the squad is gathering, and when all are out upon the field the players can be divided into groups as explained above, some groups doing one thing and some another. It is usually quite a waste of time to have the whole squad at the tackling dummy at once, because the players will have to stand idle so long awaiting their turns.

The preliminary practice of rudiments is usually followed each day by a fast signal practice. When learning new plays, each player's duties in them should be explained, and the plays run through slowly at first, until every player knows just where to run and what to do. After this it should be the aim to develop speed in the execution of the plays and in lining up after each play is made. Dummy scrimmage against a team which is making only very feeble resistance, or against a dummy defensive team such as is shown in the chapter on field equipment, is very valuable practice in teaching the players to take their correct assignments in the various plays. A short, fast, snappy signal practice is much better than a long, tedious one, and the latter should not be indulged in before a hard scrimmage because the energy and strength of the players will be so used up by it that they will be more likely to injure themselves in the scrimmage practice.

When there are not enough players on the squad for two teams to engage in a scrimmage practice, this practice can usually be had by filling the positions of the defensive team on one side of the ball, and aiming all the plays at that side.

The scrimmage should not be of more than twenty minutes duration as a rule, unless no preliminary practice is held; and no players who are suffering from injuries or who are not in good physical condition should be allowed to participate. When a player is injured another should quickly be put in his place, so that the practice may be continued without delays. The practice game should be made as near like a regular game as possible, in order that the players, especially the field generals, may have an opportunity to use their heads and to practice generalship.

Scrimmage practice is necessary to learn both offensive and defensive play, and should be held almost daily early in the season; but after the plays are pretty well learned scrimmage practice should be reduced because of the danger of injuries. After the middle of the season one or not more than two hard scrimmage practices should be indulged in each week. The practice periods should also be shortened or the practice made easier toward the end of the season.

The following program for a week's practice gives a fair idea of about how the squad should be handled from one game to another, assuming that a fairly hard game is played upon the Saturday preceding, and the Saturday ending the week.

FOOTBALL PRACTICE

Monday:

Punting, catching punts, goal kicking, place- and drop-kicking while the squad is gathering. Fifteen minutes.

Setting-up exercises. Ten minutes.

Squad is divided, the backs practicing tackling while the linemen practice charging. Fifteen minutes.

Linemen practice tackling and blocking while the backs practice starting. Fifteen minutes.

Ends join the squad of backs and practice receiving passes from the backs, who also practice receiving as well as passing. The other linemen practice starting. Ten minutes.

Blackboard talk, pointing out the mistakes of Saturday's game, and explaining new plays which are to be developed during the week. Twenty minutes.

Run through new plays and practice signals. Twenty minutes.

Scrimmage for the substitutes, and others who were not worked hard in the game on Saturday. The new plays are tried and regular players not in the scrimmage coach their substitutes. Fifteen minutes.

Late in the season it is a good plan to excuse the regulars from Monday practice after a hard game on Saturday.

Tuesday:

Punting, catching, goal kicking, place- and drop-kicking, while the squad is gathering. Fifteen minutes.

Backs practice tackling each other, while the linemen practice breaking through and charging each other. Fifteen minutes.

Linemen tackle each other, while the backs practice starting, dodging, pivoting, etc. Fifteen minutes.

Running down under punts. Twenty minutes.

Running through signals. Twenty minutes.

Scrimmage for all who are able to play. Ten-minute halves with five minutes' intermission.

Wednesday:

Same practice as on Monday and Tuesday, while squad is gathering. Fifteen or twenty minutes.

Open-field running with the ball and tackling, sometimes called "running the gauntlet." Fifteen minutes.

Backs and ends practice passing and catching passes while the linemen are receiving special instruction in opening holes, double-teaming, breaking through, etc. Fifteen minutes.

Running through signals and plays. Twenty minutes.

Scrimmage the balance of the practice period. On Tuesday and Wednesday the hardest work should be done and the scrimmage practice should be the main thing on these days.

Thursday:

Work while the squad is gathering. Fifteen minutes.

Setting-up exercises. Fifteen minutes.

Special and individual coaching for the linemen and for the backs. Twenty minutes.

Tackling and blocking. Ten minutes.

Falling on the ball and picking up a loose ball. Ten minutes.

Signal practice and dummy scrimmage and a real scrimmage in which only punting and forward pass plays are used.

Friday:

Very little or no punting for the players who may have to punt in the game.

Practice goal kicking, kicking off, passing, and catching passes.

There should be some starting, tackling, and charging practice, a rather short but snappy signal or dummy scrimmage practice, but no real scrimmage.

A dummy defensive scrimmage against the plays which the opponents are expected to use should be held. In this the duties of every man are pointed out by the coach.

Rehearse the interference in running back kickoffs.

The practice on Friday should be shorter and much easier than on other days so that the players will be fresh and fully rested for the game the following day.

This weekly program assumes that about two hours are available for practice. If a shorter time is available about the same amount of work can be done by hustling the players and keeping them on the jump, allowing no loafing or fooling.

Some coaches make the mistake of devoting nearly all their attention to the regular team, neglecting the second- and third-string men. When this is done the regular team is handicapped when a substitute has to be put in and in many cases the team work is ruined because the substitute does not know the plays perfectly. Just as much time and attention should be given the substitutes as is given the regulars. Substitutes are less experienced and more in need of coaching, and many of them are the ones who will have to be relied upon sometime in the future. I have known of several important games being lost because the coach had put in all his time upon his regulars and when one of the important cogs in his machine had to be replaced it failed to function properly.

SYSTEMS OF SIGNALS

The signals should be simple and easily learned. Many of the smaller teams have been accustomed to numbering the players and the spaces between and outside of the players on the line, the first or second number given indicating the player who is to carry the ball and the next number indicating the place to be attacked. This is not a good system of signals for several reasons. It will generally prevent good team work, because the players, other than the one who is to carry the ball and the ones in the line where the attack is to be made, are likely to forget what they are to do, as the system compels them to figure out the play before the ball is snapped. Also this system is not elastic enough and will not permit of enough combinations. There may be two or more plays where the same player carries the ball at a certain spot in the line, the plays differing in the manner in which they are worked. Then again, under this system there is no good way to signal for fakes and forward passes, or any play where the ball is handled by more than one man other than the quarterback.

A much better plan is to have each play numbered, so that when a certain number is called all players will recognize instantly the play as a whole—not simply which man is to carry the ball and where he is to run with it, but every player's part in the play. Nearly all the best teams have adopted this plan of numbering each play, but the method of calling a certain number to the attention of the players is accomplished in many different ways. One method quite commonly used is to add the first two numbers given. If this system is used the plays should be numbered from ten upward, because so few combinations of numbers give a digital sum, although many combinations of two numbers are possible to give numbers above ten. For instance, the number of the play which the quarterback has decided to use is 12. The first two numbers he calls out can be 7-5, 5-7, 8-4, 4-8, 9-3, 3-9, 10-2, 2-10, 11-1, or 1-11. It is not necessary to use the first two numbers in using this system—it can be understood that the second and third numbers are to be added, or the first and third or last.

Another system used by many prominent teams is to have the plays numbered from ten upward, and to indicate the numbers by taking the second digit of the first number called for the first digit of the number of the play, and the first digit of the second number called to indicate the second digit of the number of the play. For instance, if the number of the play to be called is 15, the quarter calls out the numbers 21-57-33, etc. If he decides to use play number 21, he can call out the numbers 42-17-26, etc. This method of giving the signals need not be worked in exactly the manner described above: it can be understood that the second digits of the first two numbers are to form the signal number, and then 32-16-11, etc., would indicate the number 26.

Another plan for indicating the number of the play is to have a key number, and have it understood that the number following a figure containing this key number will be the number of the play: for example, let 6 be the key number, and 14 the play number to be indicated; the quarterback would then call out 25-36-14-27, etc., and the players would easily understand the signal. He might also call out 62-14-37, etc., and indicate the same play, since the key number, 6, is contained in the first number called.

The simplest method of all to use in indicating the number of the play is to have it understood that the signal number is to be the first number called, or the second number, or it may be the third number, whichever is decided upon. Either this last method, or the one in which a key number is used, or the one using the second digit of the first number and the first digit of the second, I believe to be better than the others mentioned, because of their greater simplicity. There should be no thought or mental calculation required of the players in figuring out the signal number, because no matter how simple the calculation may be, it will draw the players' attention away from the game for an instant or more, and so interfere with their playing. The signal number should be conveyed to them in the simplest manner possible, so that they catch it instantly and can devote their whole thought to the game and their part in the play as soon as the signal is given. Many teams make their system of signals too complicated, seeming to fear that the opponents will be able to figure out their plays if their signals are simple; but as a matter of fact even the very simplest signals will rarely be fathomed by opposing players. During the first few seasons in which I coached the Indians the plays were numbered and the first number called was the signal number, and yet with a system as simple as that, no team, so far as I could judge, ever figured out the Indians' signals.

Very often the statement is made that a team "caught on" to the other team's signals during or before the game. But in nearly every such case it is probable instead that some player or players indicated the direction of the plays by their action or looks, or that in giving the signals the quarterback emphasized the signal number, and by repeatedly doing this, and by using a few good plays quite often, enabled the opponents to diagnose certain plays. Whenever it is feared that the opponents have solved the signals, a change can quickly be made at any time if the system is a simple one and the plays are numbered. For example, if the signal number has been the second number given it can easily be changed to the third or fourth without bothering the players at all. In fact they should be accustomed to several different methods of giving the signals, because in their practice games with the second team the latter should not know where the play is coming every time a signal is called.

The signals should be mastered thoroughly, and practiced until every player knows instinctively, the instant he hears a signal, just what he is to do in the play. The substitutes should know them as perfectly as do the regulars, so that when one of them is put into the first team the team will not be slowed up or the team work interfered with.

It is usual to number the plays so that even-numbered ones are aimed at one side of the line, while the odd-numbered plays are directed to the other. This aids in simplifying matters, and if any player does not happen to remember the play, he will at least know at which side of the line the play is to be directed.

The Huddle

In view of the growing use of the huddle system of giving signals, a discussion of its merits and its disadvantages should be of interest.

When the huddle was first tried out by a few teams several years ago, a howl went up from the fans and the newspaper critics that this method slowed up the game. Several prominent coaches experimented and gathered statistics on various games, and it was proved that just as many, and in most cases more, plays were run off in the games in which the huddle was used than in those in which the regular signal method was in use.

Of course, the speed with which the plays are gotten off varies a great deal under either system, but there is absolutely no doubt but that a team using the huddle system can get off its plays just as fast as it can by the old system, provided the players have practiced the new method and do not use up time unnecessarily. Football audiences not used to the huddle get the idea that the players gather together after each play to confer and talk things over, but the only real purpose should be to get the signal from the field general. Since all the plays are numbered the players only need to get their heads together to hear one number given, whereas in the old system several numbers have to be called in a loud tone of voice so that they can be heard above the noise and cheering of the crowd. Huddling to talk things over should be done sometimes when time-out is being taken, but never between plays.

The great noise at big games is the strongest argument in favor of the huddle system. The cheering is so loud and so continuous and the crowds are so close to the playing field that at times it is almost impossible for the players to hear the signals under the old system, and many games have been lost by some mixup or failure to hear the signal at a crucial time, usually when a team is threatening to score. At such times the supporters of the team about to score are likely to turn loose a bedlam of cheers and exhortations, making it most difficult for the players to hear the numbers shouted by their field general. By using the huddle system each player can hear the signal plainly, and misplays due to misunderstanding of the orders given are less likely to occur.

Another advantage of the huddle is the fact that the players go into their positions knowing what the play is to be, and they can adopt slightly different positions or stances best suited to the plays to be executed, whereas under the old system sharp and observant defensive players are very apt to note some slight change in the stance of certain players after the signal is given, which tips off the play.

The great disadvantage of the huddle is that the play has to be called without knowing in what formation the defense will be, whereas under the old system the field general has a chance to look over the defense to the formation his team is in and can often select a play to hit a certain spot or hole which looks to be unguarded. But this seeming advantage can be and often is nullified by the defensive players' changing their positions after the signal is given.

The huddle makes it unnecessary for the players to learn complicated systems of signals, prevents scouts from learning their opponents' signals, and, most important of all, prevents the noise and tumult from interfering with a team's play.

Many prominent teams are using the new system, and it is bound to come into quite general use soon.

Starting Signals

Quite a number of teams use starting signals when in possession of the ball, in order that the players may not have to wait for the ball to be snapped as their signal to start. In this way they get off with the ball, instead of after it is put in play. This is especially advantageous for the linemen because it gives them an instant's start on their opponents, who have to watch the snap of the ball or the start of the offensive team, giving the linemen of a team using a starting signal a chance to get the charge on their opponents. Another big advantage of a starting signal is that the players do not have to be in a position from which they can see the ball.

However, unless a starting signal is well planned and thoroughly mastered it may prove a hindrance instead of an advantage if the players get off raggedly or if the ball is ever passed at the wrong time. It should be obvious that a starting signal must be such that the team using it will know when the ball is going to be put into play and the opponents will not. If a team always starts on a certain signal, say on the second number or on the word "Hike" or "Hep," the opponents can charge on that signal also, and no advantage is gained. The word "Hike" is a good and simple starting signal providing some plays go on the ball without any signal, some on "Hike," and some on a second "Hike." Such a system will keep the opponents guessing and they cannot know when to charge except by watching the ball. Another similar method would be to use the word "Hike" for about one-third of the plays, "Hike—let's go," starting on "go," for another third, and for the other plays using "Hike—let's go—hike," starting on the second "Hike."

SYSTEMS OF SIGNALS

Another system quite generally used is to get the signal for the play and the signal to be used for the start in the first series of numbers the signal-giver calls. Then after a short pause he gives a second series of numbers for the start. For instance, we will say that the play signal is indicated by the last digit of the first number and the first digit of the second number, and the starting signal is to be indicated by the last digit of the last number. Then 21-93-52 would indicate play 19, and that the starting signal would be the second number of the starting series.

The play number itself may indicate what the starting signal is to be. For instance, it can be understood that on all play signals below 20 the starting signal is to be the first number of the starting series, all plays in the twenties are to start on the second number, plays in the thirties on the third, and in the forties on the fourth number. This is a very good system either when the signals are called by a series of numbers which all can hear or when the huddle is used. In the huddle all that would be necessary for the field general to do under this system would be to say "19"; that indicates play 19 and the players understand that the starting signal is the first number because the signal number is below 20.

Whatever system of starting signal is used, it should be such that the players get off together, and my experience has been that they get off less raggedly, to a more unified start, when they cannot anticipate when the word or starting number is going to be shouted. If they can anticipate it some of the players are inclined to beat the starting signal and the timing of the plays is all disarranged. If either the second or the third number is the starting signal and the man giving the signal rushes the numbers, calling them rapidly, some of the men will start the instant he begins calling numbers. The starting series should be given with a pause between each number, and single digit numbers should be used. There should be fully a second's pause between each number.

Players should be warned continually not to try to anticipate or beat the starting signal, because by so doing they cheat themselves by throwing the timing of the plays all out of order and by incurring frequent penalties for being in motion before the ball is put in play.

SCOUTING

Scouting in football during the season is a term and a practice which is not thoroughly understood by the general public, and for this reason scouting has been subjected to much needless criticism.

Nearly every football coach has a competent and trustworthy football man who makes it a point to see each of the strongest rival teams play in at least one game in order to note the opponents' style of offense and defense and general style of play. Unusual formations are also set down carefully. Some of the football heads at the larger universities have in past years possessed very elaborate and rather expensive scouting systems.

They would assign scouts to watch a certain team in every game it played. In this way it was possible to obtain accurate diagrams of virtually every play the opponents used and also to report the exact system of defense. Furthermore, the weak spots in each opponent's team could be noted. It was the scout's special duty to see just how the strongest plays were run off. Individual defects were also noted.

With all this information in the hands of the head coach he knew just how to attack his opponents and how to circumvent their strongest plays.

Fortunately few colleges can afford such elaborate systems of scouting, and it is doubtful if the results obtained by these means are worth the trouble and expense involved. The customary scouting system is to have one man on the staff who sees at least one game played by each of the strongest teams on the schedule. In this way a good football man can usually gather enough information for the team he represents to enable it to meet the general style of play in an intelligent manner.

All any coach needs to know about the opposing team can be discovered in one hard game, because every team, no matter how hard its coach may try to deceive his opponents, will play in about the same general style in every hard game. Efforts are often made to deceive the opposing scouts and to develop and save something new for the big games, but nine times out of ten this new stuff will not work simply because the team using it has not tried it out on a strong opponent. Lack of experience in using the new plays more than nullifies the advantage of taking the opponents by surprise.

The team which goes right ahead and in all the games uses everything the coach has given it, regardless of whether or not scouts of opposing teams are watching, will get the needed experience in working its plays and will be able to determine which of these are strongest. In this way a team can do more deadly execution with its strong plays, even though they are known, than it could with new and practically untried surprise formations.

Most successful coaches use the same general style of play from year to year, gradually making slight changes in the plays as experience dictates. As a rule one or two new plays are added to the repertoire, and perhaps the same number—those which have not proved successful—are discarded.

Nearly every coach has a system of his own which he has developed gradually from the time he first started to coach and which varies but little from season to season.

The success of the older and more experienced coaches has been in developing a style of play which the opposing teams and coaches may know almost as well as they do themselves, but which nevertheless are hard to stop because they are based on the most elementary scientific principles of football. These formations have proved their worth in many a hard-fought battle, and the plays which have failed against stronger opposition have been passed into the discard.

In the inner circles of school and college athletics it is not considered unethical or unsportsmanlike to scout opposing teams to the extent of seeing them play their games. It is perfectly legitimate to do that, but in some cases the practice is carried too far.

The important things for a scout to watch for are the formations which a team is using and the basic and most effective plays from those formations. He should note the play or plays relied on when a short, sure gain is needed to make a first down, and he should note what plays are used most on first downs, because these are very likely to be the team's best ground-gaining plays. He should learn whether or not end runs are relied upon, or whether runs just inside the defensive ends are the most used and most effective plays. He should note whether forward passes are tried on any down, or only when the team is in a hole, say on third down with a long distance to go. Are short or long forward passes used most, and does the team possess a long-distance passer? He should note to what man most passes are thrown, so that this man can be watched more closely. Does the passer use much deception by looking and faking to one man and then throwing to another? He should learn about how far punts travel, how far back the punter stands, and whether he is a fast or a slow punter.

When the team being watched is on the defense he should note what style of defense is used. Is the line low and always charging through, and do the ends play a cautious or a smashing game? Does the center play out of the line? Do they use a box or a diamond backfield defense? He should determine if possible whether a zone or a man-to-man defense to passes is being used. Who rushes the passer, and who covers the flat territory? Which of the backs are the weakest defenders against passes?

He should note where the defense seems to be weakest by watching where the other team gains the most ground. Do they rush the punter or block in the line, and is their punt receiver a good handler of punts and good at returning them? He should note how the kick-offs are returned and whether or not their kick-off man puts distance in his kicks or is a weak kicker.

Any unusual or freak formations should be noted and their best plays—the ones they use most—should be diagrammed.

If the opponents use a shifting style of play the scout should find out whether or not they play some plays without shifting and whether or not they sometimes use a double shift.

PSYCHOLOGY

"Old Man Psychology" has probably won and lost hundreds of games every season, and he will go on doing the same thing in the years to come. The coaches who are able to thwart him when he is likely to get in his deadly work, and who are able to enlist his valuable services, are the ones who will prove successful over a period of years.

A football team may be composed of the very best material, the men may be in the pink of condition and excellently coached, and yet it may be outplayed and defeated by a much inferior team composed of players who go into the games in the right attitude of mind. This correct attitude of mind is called a determined fighting spirit, and the team which has it, other things being equal, will always be the victor.

A team may be miserably coached and physically unfit, but if it has this determined fighting spirit which brooks no defeat it will subdue a much better team which goes into the game feeling confident of victory and thinking no special effort need be put forth to win.

This feature of football is so well understood by most coaches that every effort is put forth to keep their teams from becoming overconfident, and nothing is left undone to get the players keyed up to the realization or belief that they will have to put into every play every ounce of strength and every bit of speed they have if they expect to win.

In spite of these efforts, many games are lost needlessly by reason of overconfidence and demoralization as a result of meeting unexpected strength and determination in the opposing team. It is very often the case that the coach is as much at fault as the players, because he too may regard another team as easy prey, and make no special preparation for the game nor make any effort to arouse his players to put forth their own best efforts. The attitude of mind of the coach is bound to be noticed by the players, and if the coach appears assured of an easy victory an air of confidence and self-satisfaction and invulnerableness is sure to pervade the whole squad.

The older and more experienced coaches are less liable to be caught napping than the younger, greener ones, because the older men have all suffered unexpected and humiliating defeats at the hands of supposedly weaker opponents. They are more likely therefore to be on their guard against the old rascal Overconfidence, who is always plotting the downfall of the supposedly unbeatable team.

Confidence is a fine thing to possess in many sports, but not in football.

A coach who underestimates the strength of his team's opponents and overestimates the power of his own team is a fool, and his team is bound to get some unnecessary setbacks; and a team whose players are in a self-satisfied mood, who think they are going to have a very pleasant afternoon when they meet a supposedly inferior foe, is courting disaster.

When a team goes out and gathers in a goodly number of scalps without any setbacks, the critics, and especially the local sporting writers, are inclined to hail it as a world-beater. The players begin to believe they are invincible and that they do not need to train or practice very hard. They take a day off once in a while or come late to practice. Perhaps they slyly break the training rules, and the coach has a hard time getting any satisfactory work out of them. Then look out! The rival team has been coming fast! The players on it realize they are going up against an unbeaten team. The coach and players put forth extra effort and go into the game imbued with a do-or-die spirit which fairly doubles their efficiency and playing strength.

The wonderful aggregation of unbeaten players realizes too late that they are up against the real thing, and they cannot pull themselves together in time to stave off defeat. A defeat under the above conditions will benefit a team, provided there are other and more important games yet to be played, because it puts the players in a frame of mind to receive coaching instructions and to work and train faithfully, and it imbues them with the desire to retrieve themselves in the games to come.

Not only is it important that the team as a whole be so handled that it will be in the right frame of mind to put forth its best efforts, but each individual member of the team should be studied and his mental make-up correctly sized up by the coach.

There are all kinds of temperaments among the players on a team. Some are high-strung, nervous, and excitable, while others have an easy-going, phlegmatic disposition which causes them to be inclined to take things too easy. It is no small job to get the latter class of players to put forth their best efforts at all times. As a rule they cannot be counted upon to play always at top speed, especially in a game which is not considered important. The high-strung player with the real football temperament never needs to be urged nor driven but is always doing his best in every play, in practice and in games whether easy or hard; and this type of player should be carefully handled to prevent him from overworking.

The opposite type of player, easy-going and lazy, needs to be urged and driven in practice and reprimanded for every instance of loafing or of indifferent play. It takes work and strategy on the part of the coach to get the best results from this type of player, but I have often seen an apparently hopeless case of laziness and indifference suddenly changed to an irresistible, powerful force. It may have been that the player heard it whispered about that he was a quitter, or it may have been that on a certain day he happened to be feeling extra fine and played so well that his work drew forth praise from the coaches, applause from the stands, or favorable comments in the newspapers, and he then for the first time realized his powers and the joy and satisfaction of wholehearted effort and its results.

There have been players who dubbed along indifferently on the scrub team until their senior year, and then suddenly caught the spirit of the game and made varsity players of All-American caliber. Football is our most strenuous game. It takes the strenuous boy or young man to play it, and the player who cannot be depended on to give his very best effort in every play stands little chance of winning a place on the team unless there is a scarcity of dependable football material.

OFFENSE

My advice to high-school and minor college coaches is as follows: Use a few simple but strong plays perfectly worked up and do not spend a lot of valuable time on a large number of plays which, by reason of the short season and lack of experience of the squad, can only be half-baked and of doubtful value.

From my observation and what I have heard from other coaches and from high-school players themselves, I am convinced that nine out of ten high-school teams are burdened with a much too complicated system of offense. A good offense is not made up of tricky, complicated plays but of a few substantial plays perfectly worked up, in which every man, after weeks of practice, knows exactly what to do and how to do it.

High-school boys think that the big university teams are successful because they have wizard coaches who teach their teams elaborate and intricate plays. But the big university teams are good because they are composed of experienced players who have been coached well in the rudiments—who know how to tackle and block, and who have been taught a few strong plays which their coaches have found, perhaps by many years of experience, to be sure ground gainers when every man does his part in the plays. No team can get anywhere if it depends almost wholly upon tricks or forward passes. A team to be a winner must have the old punch which puts over a few simple plays with so much speed and so much hitting power that the defense cannot resist its force or the cleverness with which the plays are executed.

I do not mean to say that forward passes should never be resorted to. Every team should have three or four good forward pass plays, and perhaps six can be worked up sufficiently well to be useful; but more than this number is wasted energy and four good passes will be found to be much better than a dozen which can be only imperfectly mastered. Neither do I say that no trick plays should be used, for a good trick play used occasionally makes the opponents a bit wary and nervous; but no great reliance should be placed on tricks and only two or three should be taught any team. One of our most successful university coaches uses only about a dozen or fifteen plays, but these are so perfectly worked up and have such power in them that his teams always rank near the top at the end of each season.

From what I have seen I should say there are too many shift plays used by high-school teams. Shift plays are the hardest to execute of any system of offense and even if carefully and perfectly worked up they have no advantage over plays from a set formation. It is all right to have an unbalanced line or a one-sided formation, but plays which involve a quick shift of players should not be attempted by high-school teams. The shift is discussed more fully at the end of this chapter.

If I were coaching a high-school team I would use a standard formation such as Formation A in this book, and I would give the team about four line-plunging plays, an off-tackle play to either side, an end run to either side, and a criss-cross or reverse play with interference to take out the end instead of attempting to fool him. These would be my running plays from the close formation. From punt formation I would have a line buck to either side and a wide run to either side. I would have a short and a long pass to either side from punt formation and probably one down the center.

I think most high-school teams neglect the rudiments and spend too much time in running through signals or plays. No plays are any good unless the players know how to start quickly, how to charge and block, and how to handle the ball; practice in these things would be of much greater advantage than would a lot of time put in on fancy plays. Also it should be realized that a good defense is just as important as a good offense, and more time should be put in at tackling than most high-school players devote to this important feature of play. Eleven good, sure, and deadly tacklers are never going to be beaten very badly even if they have no offense at all.

I have noticed also that there is a tendency on the part of many high-school coaches to use their heaviest men in the backfield. This is a mistake, because the best backs in the world cannot gain when they are behind a weak line. My experience has convinced me that a strong line is more important than a strong backfield. It is all right to use one heavy man behind the line if he is fast enough to do the heavy line-plunging and is a good man both in the interference and in backing up the line on the defense; but I would use the other big men in the line.

College and university teams which are composed of fairly experienced players can master a more complicated system of offense than can the school teams, but even with such teams the tendency of many coaches is to have too many plays. In the minor, easy games a large number of plays are not needed, and in hard games in which the teams are evenly matched a team will have the ball less frequently, and when on offense will want to use only its very best plays because it will probably find that only a select few will prove effective against a very strong opposition.

Every team's offense should consist of a limited number of first-class plays, perfectly mastered, and varied enough to enable it to meet any style of defense under all sorts of conditions and to take advantage of any weakness which might develop in the defense of opposing teams. No team should depend upon one style of attack alone. The offensive strength should consist of straight, powerful line plays, end runs, and off-tackle plays with perfectly formed interference, two or three fake plays which have some power in them and do not depend entirely upon deceiving the opponents, a few good forward pass plays, and several plays from the punt formation. These should be combined with ability to kick field goals, while a quick punt from a regular running formation is often of value and should occasionally be used when the ball can be punted over the defensive backs' heads.

Trick plays are useful to add variety to the attack and to keep the opponents guessing, thus aiding the regular plays. Perhaps a trick play will occasionally result in a long run, but no great dependence should be placed in them and only a few good ones should be taught the players.

In choosing plays to be diagrammed in this book care has been taken to select only those which have been found to be effective in actual competition against strong opposition, and I believe the list is varied enough to enable any coach or team to select from it a powerful, scientific, and varied offense which will succeed against the defense of any team in its class.

There are sixteen plays diagrammed from Formation A, and the same number from Formation B. This will give thirty-two plays from each formation if the same plays are worked from both right and left formations. Note, however, that it would not be advisable to work some of the passes from the left formation because of the difficulty a right-handed passer has in running to the left and passing. There are twelve plays diagrammed from the punt formation.

About twenty, or no more than twenty-five plays are all any team should have, and I would advise users of these plays to select their offense from either Formation A or Formation B (but not from both of them), and from the punt formation.

The Shift

The shifting style of offense wherein either the backfield or the line, or both line and backfield, quickly shift their positions before a play is made has been unduly popularized because of the success which a very prominent coach has had with this style of play, and because of his advocacy of it at the summer coaching schools which he has conducted in all parts of the country during the past few years. The chief exponent of this style of play claims that the shifting style of offense is better because it is harder to stop. There would be no answering that argument if it were true, but there is nothing to prove the claim except the unusual success of the teams which this famous coach has been turning out annually. Is it not possible that this team's fine record might be due more to the ability of their coach in teaching correct fundamentals, in developing a strong defense, and in getting the best possible results from the excellent material he has had to work with, rather than to the shifting style of offense which he has used? And is it not possible that his teams would have had as good or better success using a set formation instead of the shift?

To prove that the shift is not necessary to achieve success on the gridiron, we only need to look at the records for the past several years. Only a small fraction of the leading teams of each year have used the shifting style of attack. If it were true that the shift is harder to stop, all coaches with any brains would be using that system, but as a matter of fact the majority of the better coaches are not using it—proof that they do not think it is the best form of attack. If the majority of the most experienced leading university coaches do not use the shifting style with their experienced players, then surely high-school coaches should not attempt to use it, because it is so much more complicated and so much harder to develop than is the standard set method of play.

In past years I have given the shifting style of play a thorough trial, and each time I have tried it I have found to my own satisfaction, and to the satisfaction of the players and of my assistants, that the same plays gave better results from a set formation than they did when worked by shifting into the different formations quickly before each play, and that the physical exertion and the amount of practice required was much less.

The main value of the shift lies in gaining momentum, which has been for some years against the rules; and now that there must be a one-second stop, and since the penalty for having men in motion, or for failing to come to a stop, has been increased from five to fifteen yards, the main value of the shift has been destroyed, and it is bound to be even less effective than it ever was.

In this style of play the shifting players are off balance when the ball is put in play, while in the set formation they are dug in and in a position to exert their full strength. In a shift attack the offensive team never knows in what position their opponents are going to be, because the defensive players shift with the offensive team, whereas in the set formation the players of the attacking team see where their opponents are, they know whom they are to block, and they have time to figure out how best to handle their assignments.

In a shifting attack no satisfactory method has been devised to prevent the opponents from outcharging the offensive team, because the defensive players quickly learn the timing of the shift, and can so time their charge that they can either beat the ball or at least get off with it. But in a set formation with a good starting signal the offensive team can always get the charge on their opponents. Against a shifting attack the defense can always secure the advantage by shifting more than the attacking players, because while the momentum gained by shifting is an aid to plays going in the general direction of the shift, it is a handicap to the execution of plays going in the opposite direction, and therefore the weak-side plays of a shifting team are always decidedly ineffective and are seldom used except as a threat. In a set formation the players can start to either right or left with equal ease and effectiveness, and their plays to the weak side can be worked up just as successfully as the plays to the strong side of their formations.

Another argument used in favor of the shift is that it looks pretty and is spectacular, but the main object of offensive football should be to gain ground rather than to work up a rhythmic fancy movement such as is necessary for the success of a Russian toe dancer, and I firmly believe in dispensing with the Pavlowa stuff and getting right down to the business in hand— that of gaining ground with the least possible fuss and feathers and with as little waste effort as possible.

FORMATION A[1]

This offensive formation has often been referred to as the "Carlisle formation" because it was first used by the Indians. With slight variations it probably has been copied more by other coaches than has any other formation ever developed, and it has come to be the most generally used. I have used this formation or variations of it ever since pushing and pulling the runner was prohibited in 1906. Before that time it was customary to mass the backs behind the line and even bring one or two heavy linemen back, so as to be able to hurl a mass of men at any spot in the defensive line. The idea was to get behind the man with the ball and shove and jam him through the line, or let him jump in the air feet first while the other men shoved him over the line and helped him by dragging him along. The best line-buckers in those days were men who could keep their feet and depend upon the men back of them to carry them forward. The good line-bucker was the man who ran high, stepped high, and actually leaned back upon the men behind him so that he could climb over the opposing line something like a man would do if he were being pushed upstairs, because it can easily be seen that if a man's feet were stopped, the push behind him would simply shove him over on his face.

When the rules were changed to prevent pushing the runner, there was no more reason for the backs being massed. Those behind the runner were of no use, and in line-bucking plays only two men, the ball carrier and a man to precede him or lead him through the hole, were needed. The use of more than one man to precede the runner was found to be inadvisable in most cases because they made the play too congested and actually were in the runner's way. Since men were not needed to push, and only two men were needed to hit the line on bucking plays, it was found to be an advantage to utilize the backs in such a way that they might be able to assist the linemen and still be in a position to precede and form interference for the runner on wide plays. So it became advisable to put one of the backs in a position to flank a tackle, thus, by making the back in a way a

---

[1] Diagram on page 140.

part of the line, giving the line an eight-man front. This idea is being carried a step further by several coaches who use a back on each side to flank both tackles, the line thus presenting a nine-man front, as is shown in Diagrams A-10, A-16, and the diagrams of plays from Formation B. This two-wing-back formation has many advantages but necessitates double passing, or having a back in motion, to get the ball from the center to the wing backs, and is therefore too complicated for use by any but the most experienced and clever players. It is especially unsuited to field conditions which make the ball slippery and hard to handle.

Therefore, for all high-school and other teams on which somewhat inexperienced players have to be used I would recommend this "A" formation. It may be found practical to vary this formation by jumping up the rear back (No. 11 in right formation), to flank the short-side tackle, as shown in Diagram A-10, on a few plays such as the reverse play and a line buck or two. This formation helps the reverse plays and also aids tandem bucks through the line, because with both tackles flanked the whole defensive line has to play somewhat wider, and so is easier to tandem through. While only two plays have been diagrammed with this change of the "A" formation any coach can easily accommodate to the change most of the plays diagrammed, since the player moved up to flank the tackle on the short side is used either to work on the tackle or to carry the ball around the opposite tackle or end. In the latter case, to get the ball from center he must be in motion before the ball is put in play or must receive it on a double pass from player 10.

This "A" formation differs from most formations of its kind generally used in that the rear or weak-side back stands about four and one-half yards behind the short-side guard (No. 2), instead of directly behind the center. By playing him there both guards can be utilized for interference to the long side, whereas if the runner stood behind the center it would be difficult indeed for the short-side guard to get ahead of him on plays outside of tackle to the long side.

No. 10, the fullback, is the man used principally for line bucking and for interfering, and should be a heavy and hard-plunging back. He plays behind the long-side guard, No. 4 in the diagram, and is about three and one-half yards back. The quarterback or interfering back (No. 9) plays about a yard and one-half behind the hole between No. 5 and No. 6. The wing back (No. 8) plays outside of the defensive tackle, no matter how wide the tackle plays, and he is about one yard back of the line.

The whole line should play what is called a "tight line," just as closely together as the rules will allow. I have found it is of some advantage for all the linemen to play with left foot advanced on right formation and right foot advanced on left formation, because it is natural for the defensive linemen to charge toward their opponent's strong side. With the feet placed as explained, and as shown in the diagrams, the offensive linemen are better braced to withstand their opponent's initial charge. The center is an exception to this rule unless he can pass the ball equally well with either foot advanced. The three backs who are behind the line stand with their feet about even; but the wing back has his outside foot advanced.

In this formation the line is unbalanced because the middle man in the line, No. 4 in the diagram, is the most valuable lineman for interference on plays going outside of tackle or around the end on either the long or short side, and he could not pull out and interfere if he first had to feed the ball to the runner.

The formation can be made by bringing over either a guard, a tackle, or an end; but in arranging the formation the most active and best interfering lineman, No. 4 in the diagram, should be stationed in the middle of the seven forwards, because, as explained in the preceding paragraph, he does more interfering than does any other lineman. The center and No. 5 in the diagram are the linemen who are seldom or never used in the interference, and the slowest lineman on the team should be placed where No. 5 is shown.

In the backfield the wing back can play that position on both left and right formation, but if both No. 11 and No. 8 are good ball carriers and are equally good at boxing a tackle it is best to have No. 11 the wing back and No. 8 the rear back on left formation, since this divides up the work of carrying the ball. If only one good running back is available he can be used as the rear or short-side back in both right and left formations.

With this formation the rear back can fade back on some

plays, or all the plays can be worked without any player moving before the ball is put in play. That is optional with the coach.

In diagramming the plays in the book I have pictured the defense in about the position a well-coached team would shift into to meet an unbalanced formation. If a defensive team does not shift over in front of the offensive team the long-side plays will go better, and if they shift farther over than shown, then the short-side plays will put them at a disadvantage.

The plays are all diagrammed from the right formation. The left formation plays can easily be determined without diagrams. If necessary these right formation plays can be looked at in a mirror to get the left formation, or they can be copied by placing a blank piece of paper under the page with carbon paper, face up, under that, and then tracing the diagrams.

Each play is diagrammed formally against the diamond defense and is pictured in perspective, or bird's-eye view, against the box defense, so that it should be easy to comprehend the formations, plays, relative distances between players, and so on, by noting the five-yard lines.

This is the formation I would strongly advise for high schools, and in fact I believe it is as good a formation as can be devised for any team. Of course the punt formation should be used for punting, and generally it is advisable to have on tap several running and forward passing plays from that formation. Such a formation and plays from it are diagrammed further on in the book.

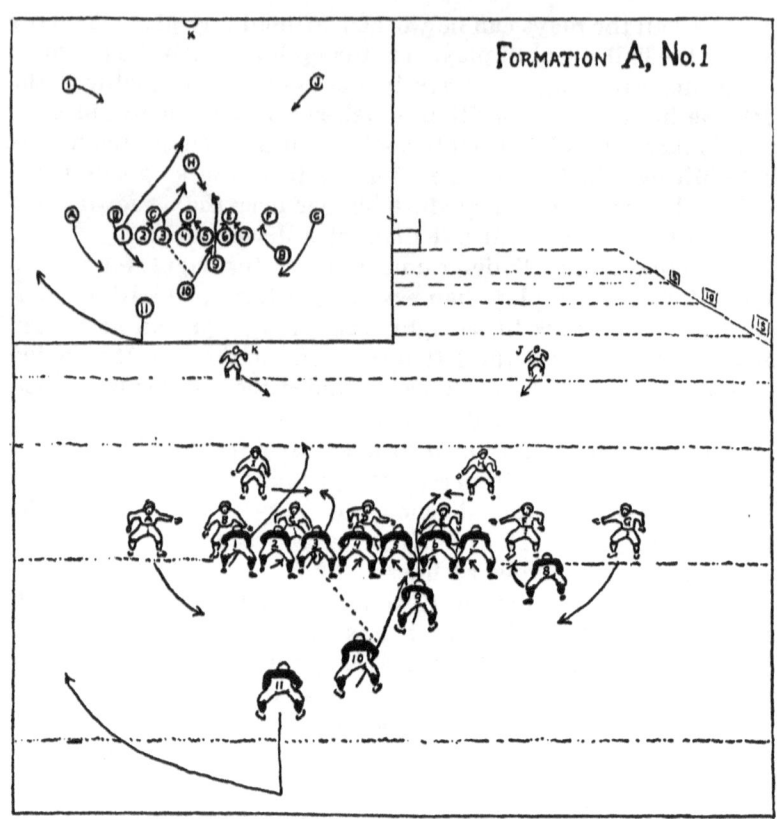

A-1: Tandem buck between defensive center and left guard. 4 and 5 double-team D, driving him backward and turning him to the left. 6 and 7 drive E backward and to the right. The arrows show how the other linemen should block. B is too far away to harm the play and 1 can go through for secondary. 3 side-swipes C and goes through also. 9 precedes the runner through the hole and blocks off the man backing up the line, and 10 follows directly behind 9, carrying the ball. 11 can either fade back, throwing up his arms as if to receive the pass, or he can run to either side to attract attention. He also watches for a fumble.

This tandem can be worked to hit between C and D, but for attacking the openings just inside the defensive tackles other plays diagrammed are better.

FORMATION A

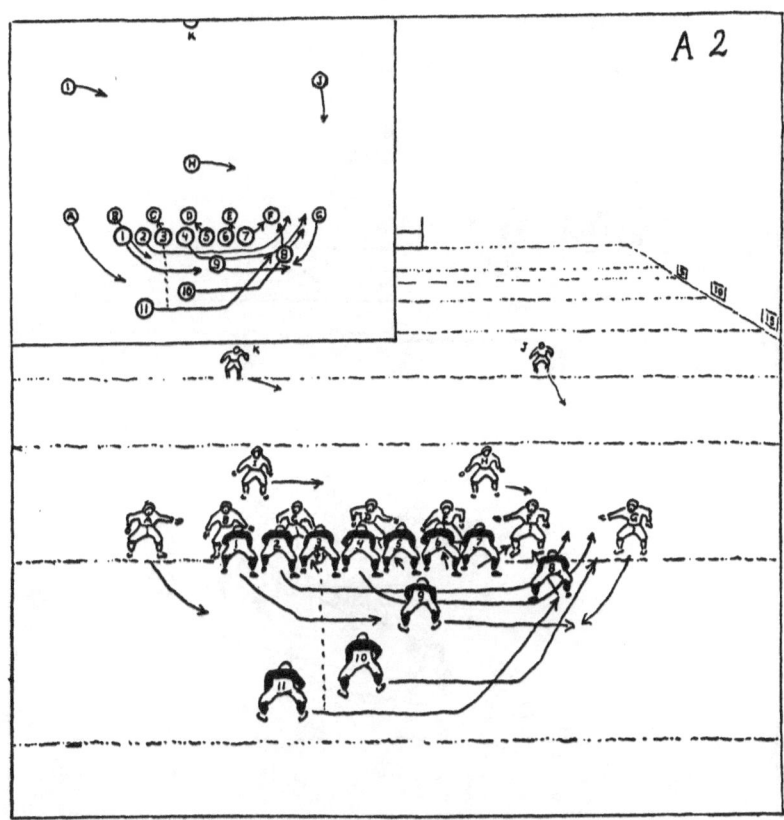

A-2: This play has been variously named the off-tackle play, short-end run, or "the three-out-and-up" play, and is one of the strongest plays ever developed. Nos. 8 and 7 turn F in. 6, 5, and 3 block E, D, and C to the left. 2 and 4 pull out of the line and turn down the field as they pass F. 9, 10, and 11 start parallel to the line as though they were going around end. This brings G in rather deep. 9 hits G and drives him out, and 10 leads 11 inside of G. 3 leads the ball to 11 by an easy lob pass. 11 and 10 take three steps out, starting with the right foot, then turn sharply up the field. This turn is made just as 9 is hitting G. 1 follows up the play as safety man.

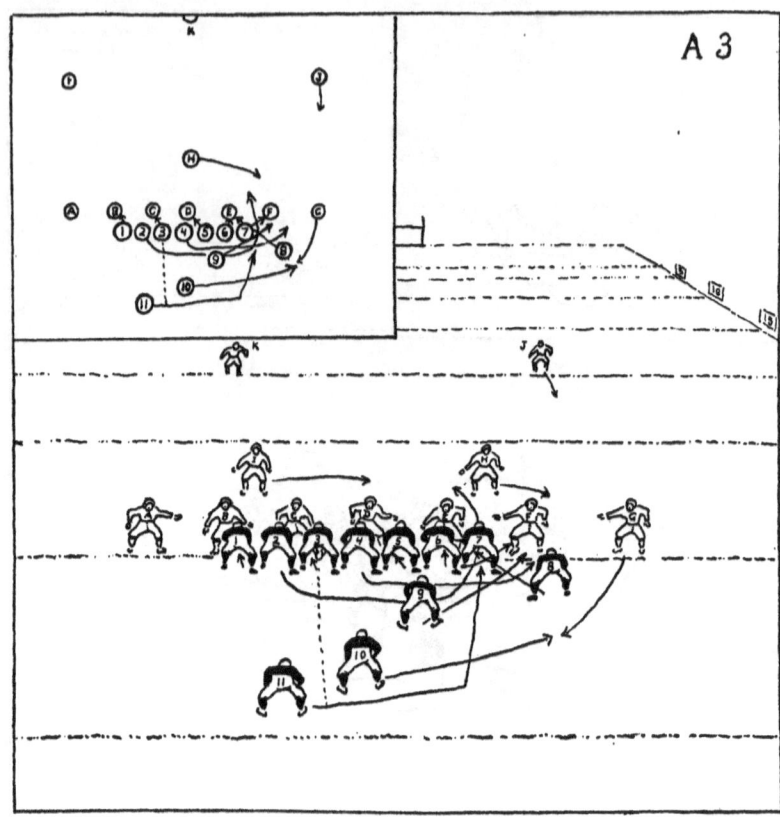

A-3: This is the "cut back" play. It starts like A-2 and looks like that play. 8 and 7 cross-block, 7 driving F out and 8 driving in behind 7 as the latter charges into F, to help 6 block E to the left. 9 assists 7 on F. 2 and 4 pull out of the line as in A-2, 4 continuing outside of F but helping to sweep him out if he advances. 2 turns inside of F and leads the runner, blocking off secondary. 10 drives G out, and 11, starting as in A-2, cuts inside of F just as 10 is hitting G. 11 should not go too fast on the first three steps because he cannot make a sharp enough turn if he starts at top speed. He should drive hard after turning.

FORMATION A

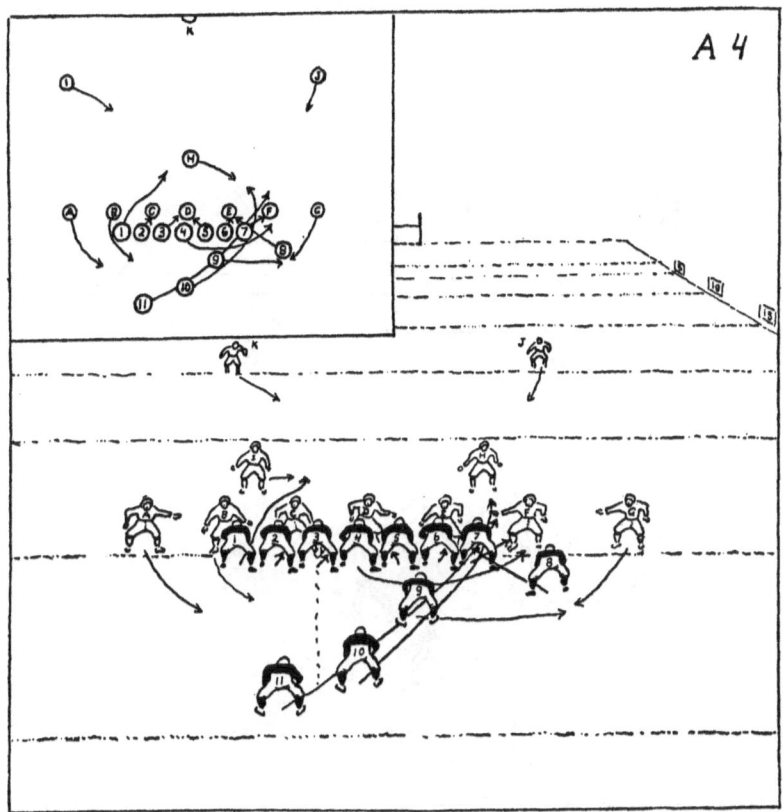

A-4: This is a powerful straight drive just inside of defensive tackle. 7 blocks F out and 4 comes out of the line and assists him. 8 cross-blocks, assisting 6 to carry E to the left. 9 blocks G out. 10 precedes 11, the ball carrier, in a driving, slanting tandem, hitting between E and F. For a sure gain of a few yards this is a better play than A-3.

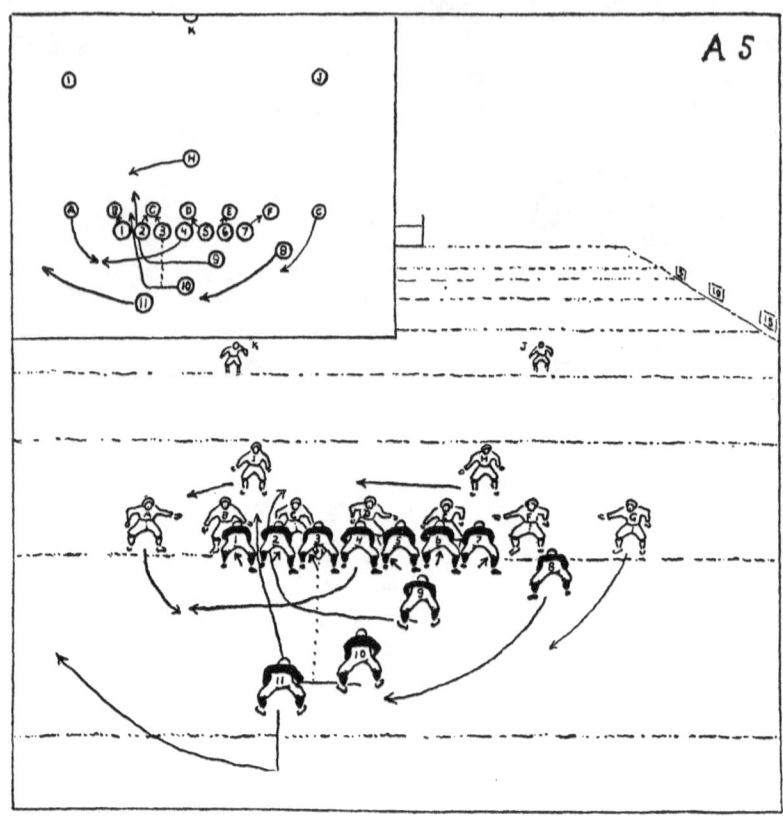

A-5: This is a very strong play for attacking the hole inside of tackle on the short side. 1 blocks B out, the deception of so many men starting as though to go outside of him causing B to charge wide. 2 and 3 block C to the left. 5, 6, and 7 stop D, E, and F. 4 pulls out and blocks A. 11 runs wide, fading back before the ball is put in play or remaining in position. 9 moves to the left, not so fast that he will bump into 4, and shoots into the hole to lead the runner and to block off secondary. 3 leads 10 in passing the ball and 10 takes two steps to the left, continuing to keep his front toward the line, taking the first step by crossing over his right foot, then stepping with the left and driving off of that foot straight ahead. 8 comes around to aid in making the defense believe it is a wide play. This play can also be worked with a fake of the ball to 8, as shown in play B-5.

FORMATION A

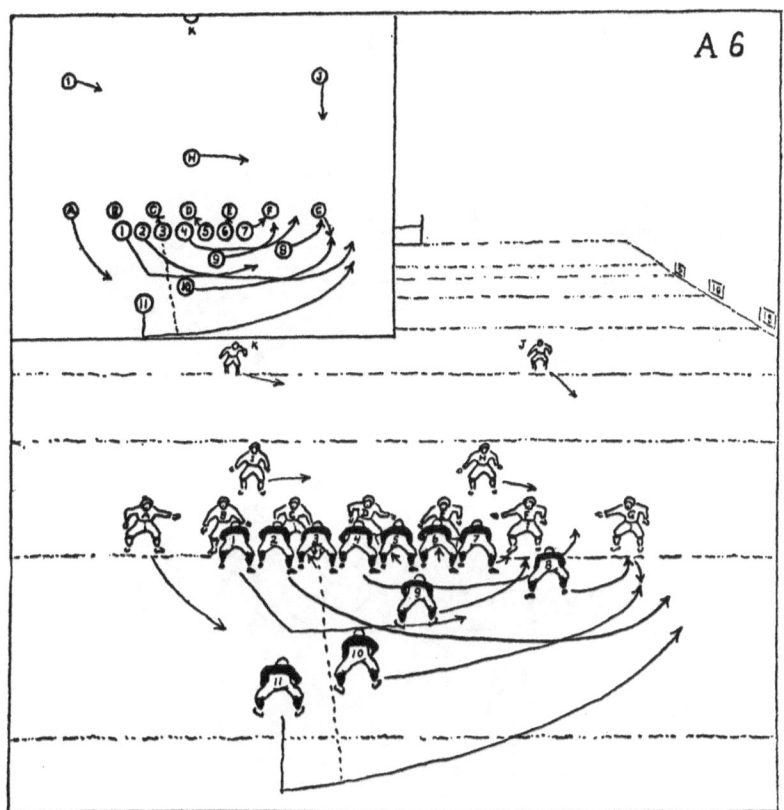

A 6

A-6: This is a very strong run around end. It is a valuable play, not only for its own merit but as it helps the other plays; because if G knows that sometimes 8 blocks him for a run outside of him he dares not play close in and that helps to make the plays inside of him go much better. 8 blocks G in, and 10 assists him, coming up on the outside of G. 9 assists 7 in blocking F in. 4 and 2 pull out of the line, 4 cutting in just outside of F and taking secondary and 2 swinging wide and leading the runner around the end. 11 fades back before the ball is snapped, or runs from his original position. The fade-back puts the runner in a better position for this play and is advisable if you are using it in some other plays.

146   FOOTBALL FOR COACHES AND PLAYERS

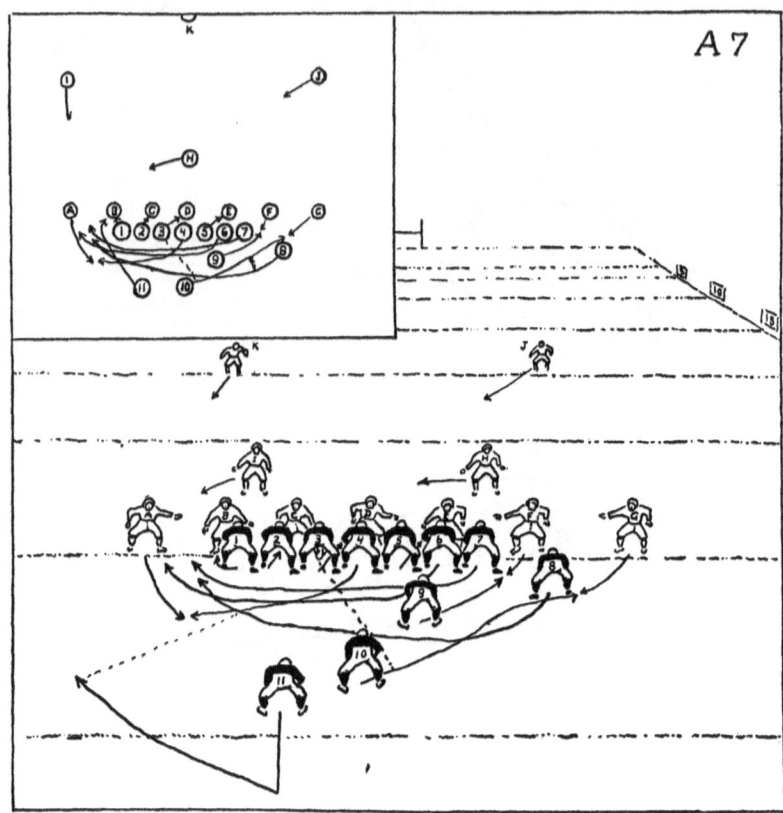

A-7: This is a reverse play and is a very strong play for attacking the weak side. It can be played by fading back 11 before the play starts and having him run wide as a threat or as an actual receiver of a lateral pass; or he can edge up a little closer to the line without attracting attention, so that he can help block B without getting in the way of 4, who comes out of the line to block A. 1 blocks B to the right and 2, 3, and 5 do likewise to C, D, and E. 9 starts to right and blocks F. 10 gets the ball from 3 and starts to the right just outside of F, handing the ball to 8 as he meets him. 6 and 7 pull out of the line and lead the runner just outside of B. The lateral-pass play shown in the picture diagram should be very valuable under the new rules, 8 being given the option of making the lateral pass to 11 or continuing with the ball. 8 will be almost facing 11 when the lateral pass is made and can lob the ball with both hands (a push pass from the chest) over the head of A if he is in the way.

FORMATION A

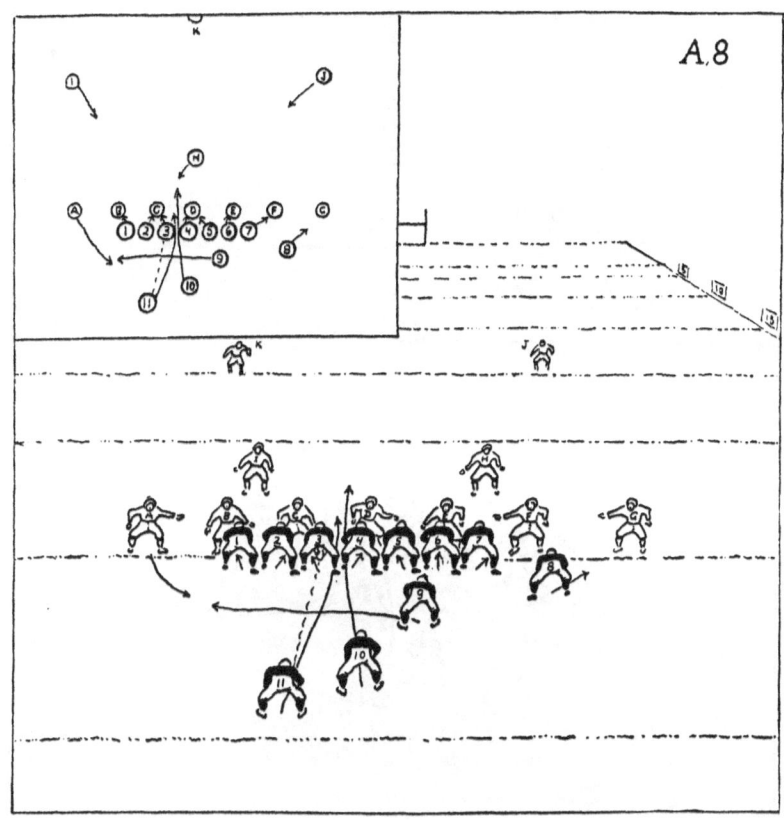

A-8: This is a good play for attacking the opening between C and D, providing 11 is a good smashing back. 2 and 3 double-team C back and to the left. 4 and 5 carry D back and to the right. The other linemen block their opponents away from the play as shown. 9 edges up close to the line and crosses in front of 10 and 11, blocking A. This somewhat confuses the defense and makes it easier to block C to the left. 10 precedes the runner, 11, in a straight-ahead tandem. The latter two pause for an instant, if necessary, so as not to bump into 9.

A-9: This is an effective and deceptive "spin-play." 10 receives the ball from center, steps to the right, and fakes the ball to 11, making a complete turn while faking, and then driving into the line outside of D. 6 pulls out of the line and blocks the end out. E will be drawn through the hole left vacant by 6, and will naturally charge as shown to head off 10 and 11. 9 hesitates and as E charges through, drives him to the right, or if E does not charge through, 9 drives straight ahead into him. 2 comes around and precedes the runner through the opening. 4 and 5 block D to the left, and 7 and 8 carry F to the right.

FORMATION A

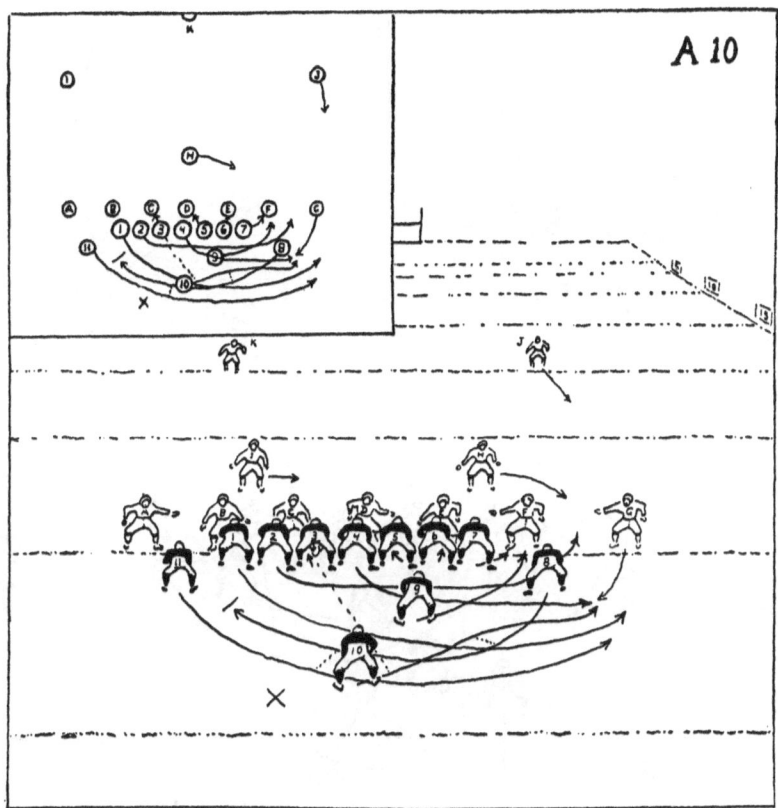

A-10: A triple-pass play around end, not so dangerous now that there is no danger of losing the ball on fumbles of the passes, the last two of which are backward or lateral passes. Before the play starts 11 jumps from his original position at X to the position shown, or if the huddle is used he takes this position when coming out of the huddle. 10 receives the ball from center, starts to the right, and hands it to 8, continuing on and blocking G. 8 hands the ball to 11 as they meet and 11 swings wide with 1 leading him around the end. 9 assists 7 in blocking F. 4 pulls out of the line and helps 10 block G. 2 pulls out and runs outside of F for interference. 6, 5, and 3 block E, D, and C to the left. Everyone starts with the snap of the ball.

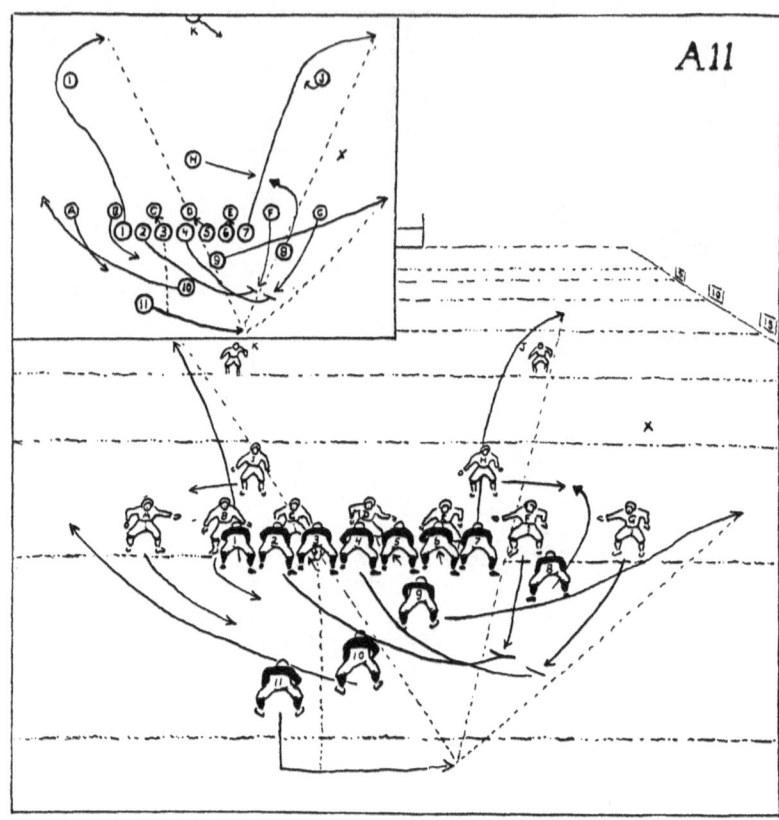

A-11: These forward passes can be played with 11 fading back before the ball is put in play or they can be played with 11 in his regular position, as shown in the upper diagram. The center lobs the ball back, leading the passer so that the latter does not have to wait for the ball before starting. This can be used as an optional pass to 1, 7, or 9, but I believe it is best to have a separate signal for each of the three passes. 11 runs to the right and back while getting ready to throw, not looking at the man he plans to throw to. 8 blocks H before the pass is made if the pass is to 9, but if the pass is going to be made to 7, then 8 runs to position marked X, so as to draw J to cover him. 2 and 4 come well back to protect the passer, and they and the passer hurry over to the right as safety men if the pass is made to 9.

FORMATION A

151

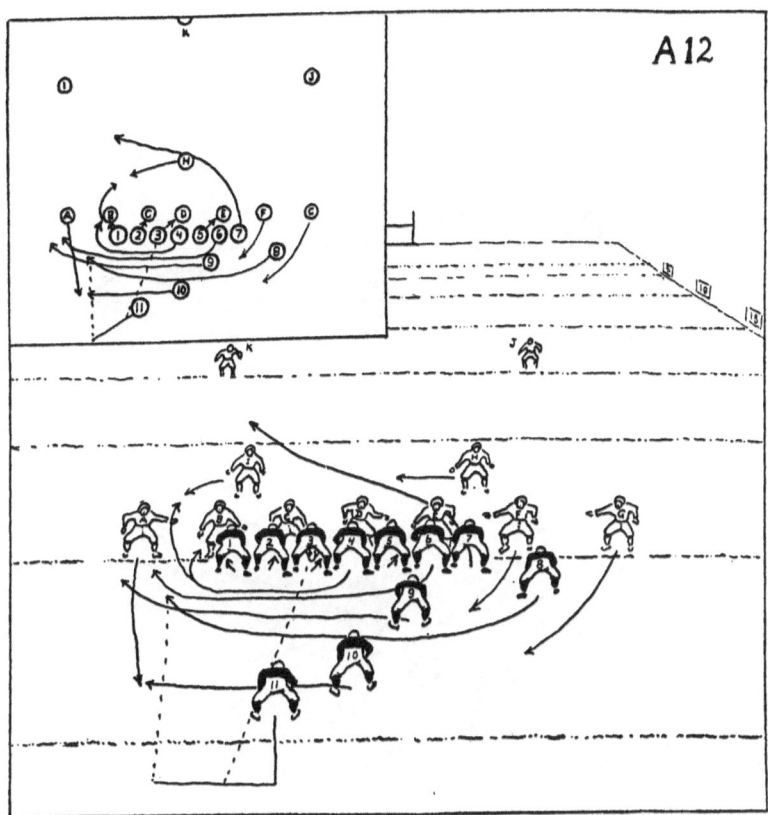

A12

A-12: Short screen-off-tackle pass to the weak side. 11 receives the ball from center and runs to the left. If he has not faded back he runs back and to the left. This usually brings the defensive end A well in to hurry or to block the pass and he can easily be put out of the play by 10. 4 comes around to help 1 block B in, if help is needed. If 1 has B blocked then 4 cuts off the first defensive back. 9 and 6 swing around outside of B to interfere for 8, who receives an easy overhand pass from 11. 7 goes through the lines and runs over as shown, making a bluff to receive the pass and thus decoying the secondary defensive men from coming up to stop the real receiver. This pass is almost absolutely safe and can be used even near your own goal. The gain depends on the run after the pass is received.

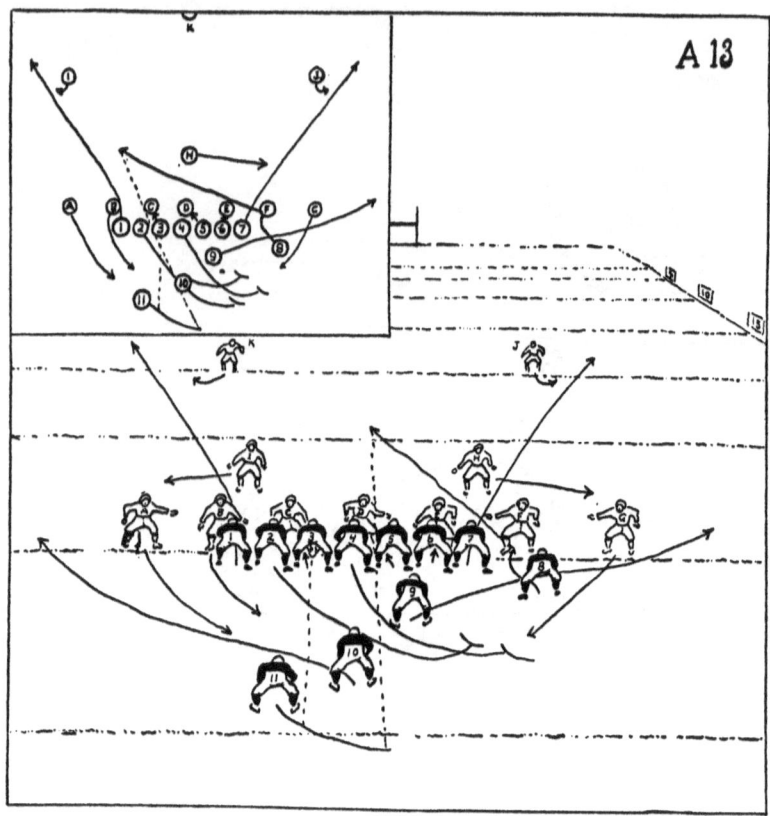

A-13: This is an excellent pass and almost a sure thing if well played against a box defense with a seven-man line. 11 gets the ball from center, runs back and to the right looking at 9, and then whips the ball quickly to 8 who has first blocked F, thus causing the defensive backs to withdraw their attention from him, there being four other eligible men to cover. Against the box defensive or a six-man line defense, 10 should run to the left to draw the close secondary-defense man on that side to cover him; but against a diamond defense with a seven-man line 10 should move to the right and protect the passer, thus making it more certain that H will run to cover 9. Against the diamond defense 8 should work over farther to the left, as shown in the upper diagram. The delay of 8 and a good bluff to 9 makes this a great pass.

FORMATION A

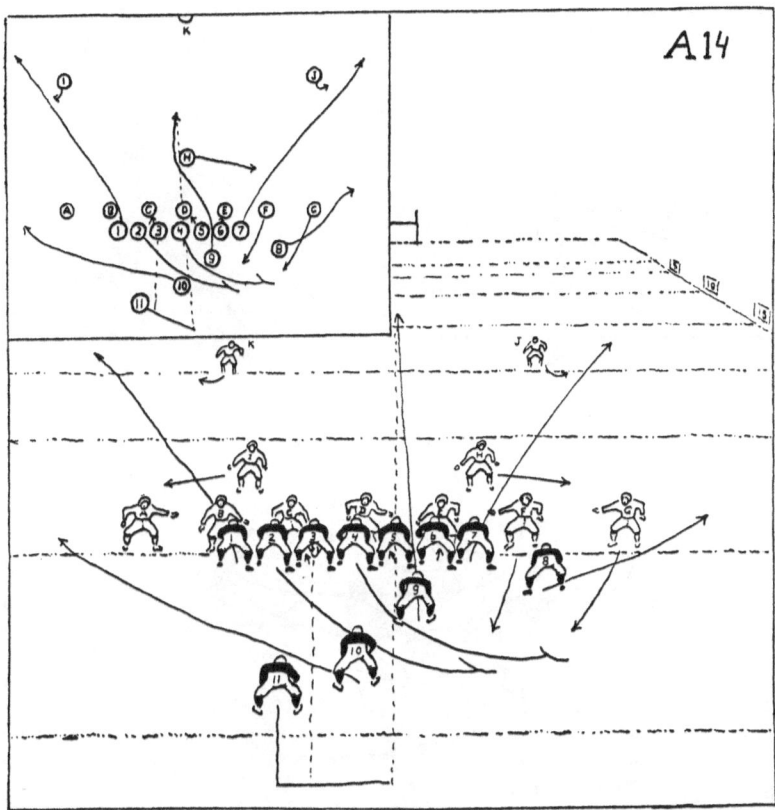

A-14: This is a fine pass against a box defense, or against a diamond defense where the safety man is playing well back. 7 and 1 run deep and wide to pull the defensive halfbacks out. 8 and 10 run out wide as shown. 9 goes straight through the line and down the middle, about twelve yards against a diamond defense, and as deep as he can against a box defense. 11 comes well back and a little to the right before throwing and 2 and 4 swing well back to protect him. The pass should be more delayed and should be thrown farther against a box defense than against a diamond backfield defensive formation.

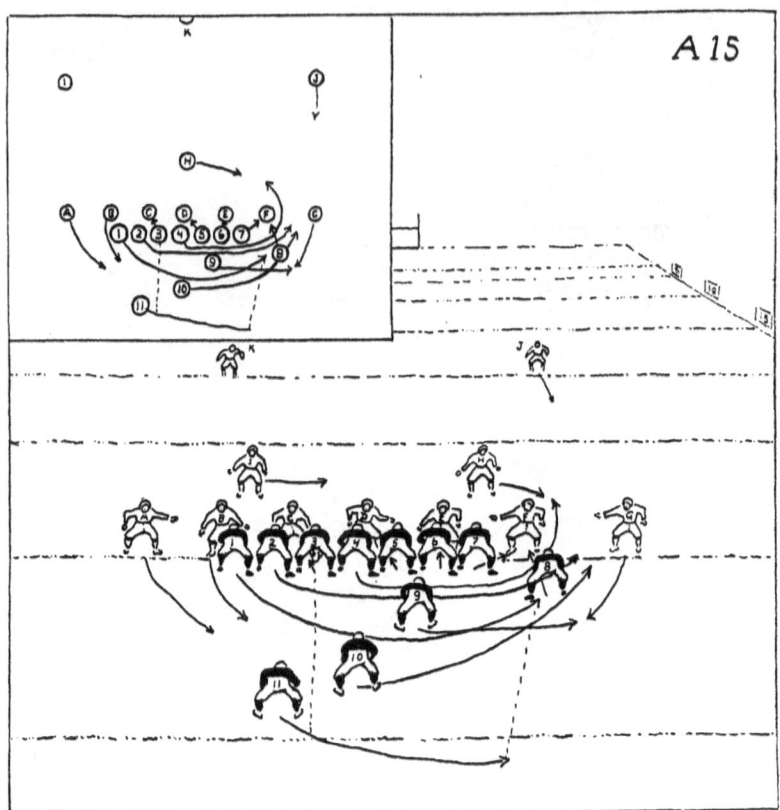

A-15: This is a pass of the same nature as A-12 but to the strong side. 11 starts wide and back so as to be more than five yards back when making the pass. This brings G in to hurry or to block the pass and he is carried out by a hard block by 9. 1 comes around and takes a short toss from 11, having 10, 2, and 4 ahead of him as interferers after he catches the pass. 8 and 7 box the tackle F to the left. This is a safe pass that can be used anywhere on the field without danger of interception.

FORMATION A

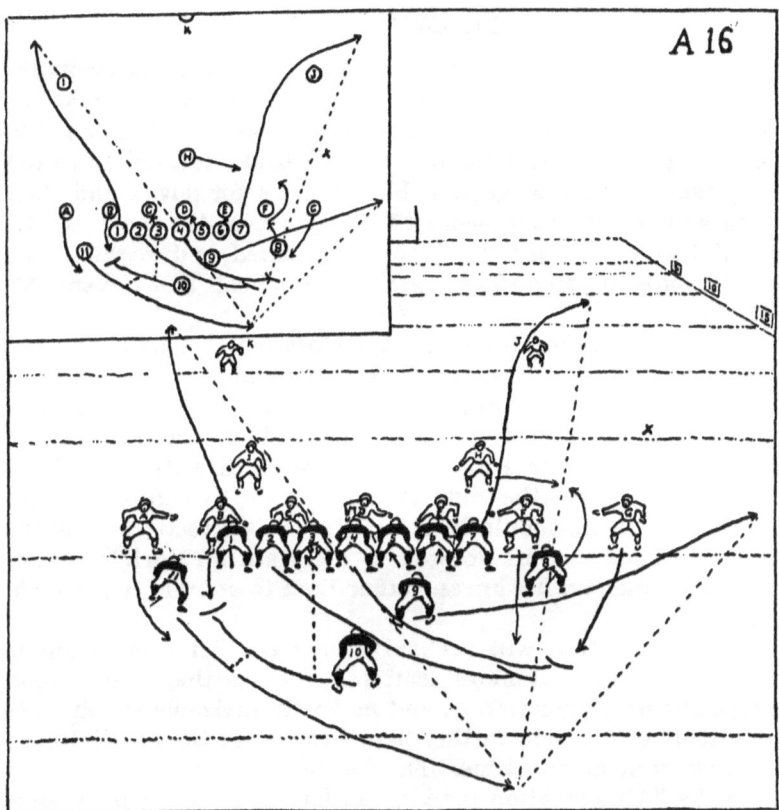

A-16: The reverse forward pass has proved a winner in many games. The two long passes shown scored touchdowns against California in '24 and enabled Stanford to tie the score in the last few minutes of the game after apparently having been beaten 20 to 6.

11 lines up as a wing back on the left and receives the ball from 10, swinging well back and passing to either 1, 7, or 9. 2 and 4 swing back for protection. If the pass is to be to 7, then 8 runs to point marked X to draw up J. If the pass is to be made to 9, then 8 cuts off H. This pass could be optional with a clever passer, but I have found it best to have separate signals for the three passes.

FORMATION B

This is a formation making use of two wing or tackle-flanking backs, and is an excellent formation for an open style of play, especially when a triple-threat man—a man who can run, punt, or pass—is available for the rear back, marked 10 in the diagrams. It is not as good as Formation A for power and close work and is not recommended for any except the most experienced teams, because it is too complicated and requires too much double passing to be practical for schools and the smaller colleges.

In this formation the line plays close together and the wing backs should play outside the defensive tackles and a yard back of the line. A heavy line-plunging back, who is also a good interferer and handler of the ball, should be in the position marked 9, about three and one-half yards directly behind the center of the line—the right guard in right formation. Player 10, the rear back, should be about six yards directly behind the ball. This player will do well to maintain an upright stance with his hands on his knees, rather than to assume the crouching stance.

This formation will probably force the defensive team to assume a somewhat more scattered defense than they would adopt against Formation A, and makes it advisable for them to play their safety man farther back because of the possibility of a quick punt at any time. The formation is somewhat better than the "A" formation for playing lateral passes, and is especially good for forward-pass plays. It has been used by Lafayette and the University of Pittsburgh with much success.

FORMATION B

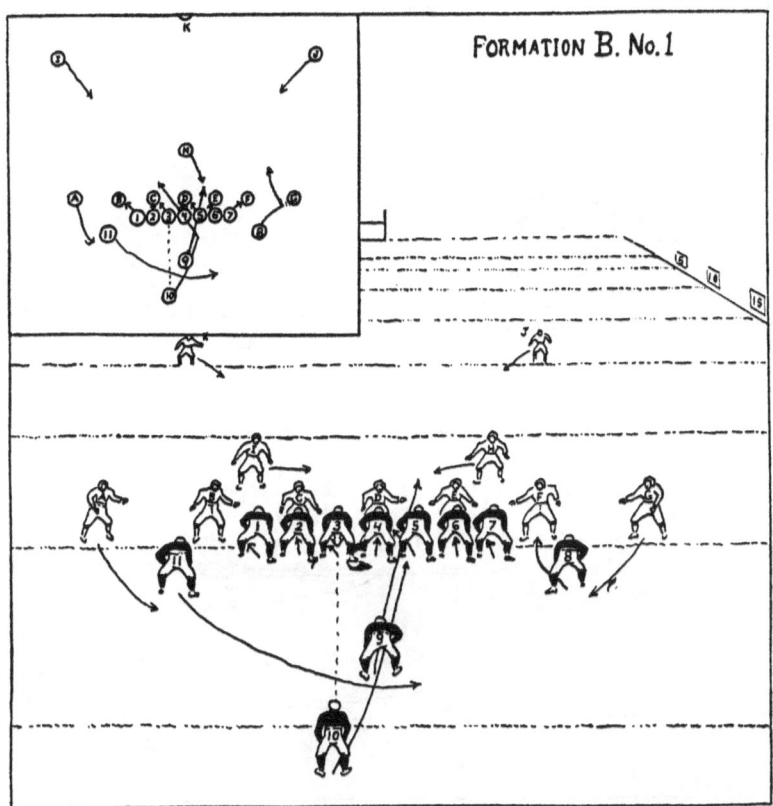

FORMATION B. No. 1

B-1: A simple and powerful play to go between defensive center and left guard. 4 and 5 double-team D; 6 and 7 do the same to E. 9 leads the runner, 10, in a tandem drive through the hole. 10 is far enough back so that he can side-step or veer to either left or right in case a hole opens up at either side; or such a move can be planned as a separate play, as shown in the upper diagram. Both the straight drive and the variation of it as shown are very effective. The arrows show the duties of all the players.

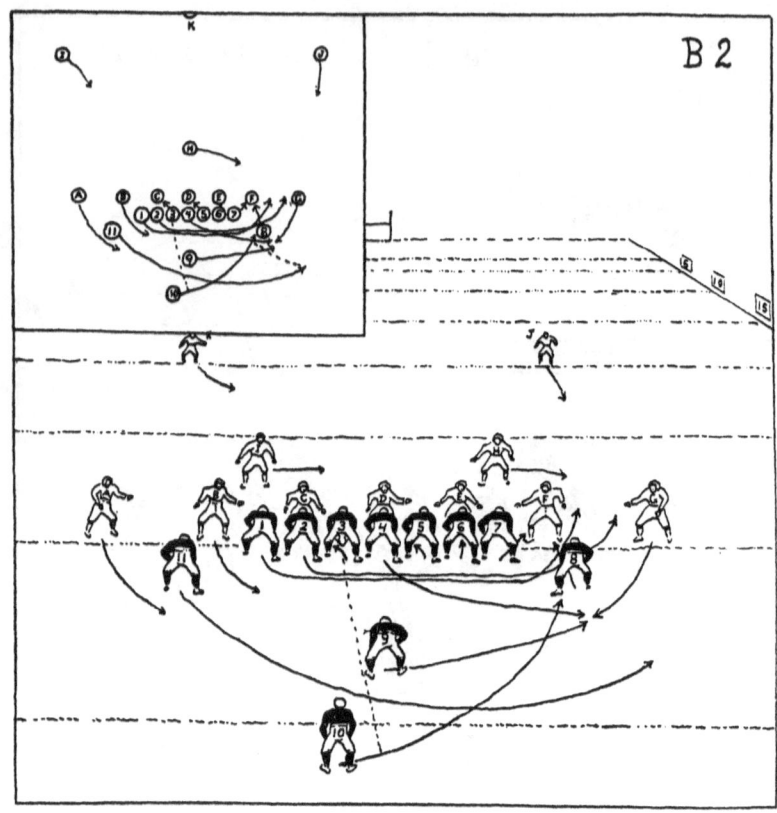

B-2: Off-tackle play or short end run. 4 and 9 block the defensive end out. 1 and 2 swing around outside of F. 7 and 8 box the tackle in. 11 swings around fast and wide and is in a position to take an easy toss backward or a lateral pass from 10, who starts rather wide and makes about a quarter-circle swing. The regular run and threat to pass to 11, and the actual pass to 11, both make excellent plays and will give the defending end a lot of trouble. Used as one play with an optional pass by 10.

If a man in motion is used, then 11, starting before the ball is passed, should help 9 on the end and 4 would swing around F, taking out H.

FORMATION B 159

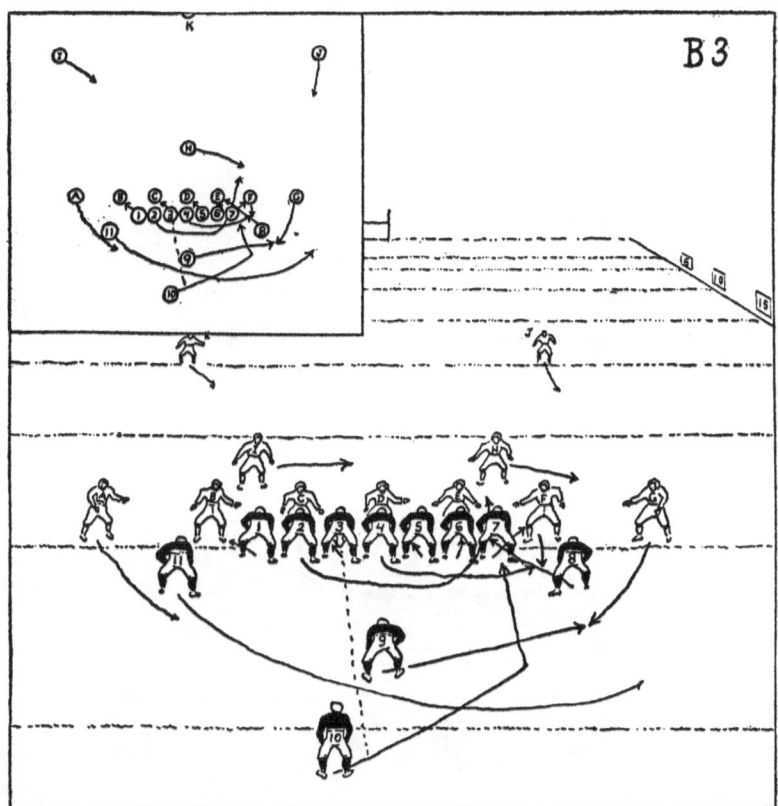

B-3: Fake off-tackle cut-back play. This play starts like B-2. 9 carries the end out. 4 swings across, helping 7 to carry the tackle out. 8 drives in behind 7 as the latter charges forward at F and cross-blocks the guard E, assisting 6. 2 swings around and leads the runner, 10, through the hole. 10 starts as in B-2 but not too fast, making a quick turn just as 9 is hitting G. 11 swings around as in B-2 to aid in the deception.

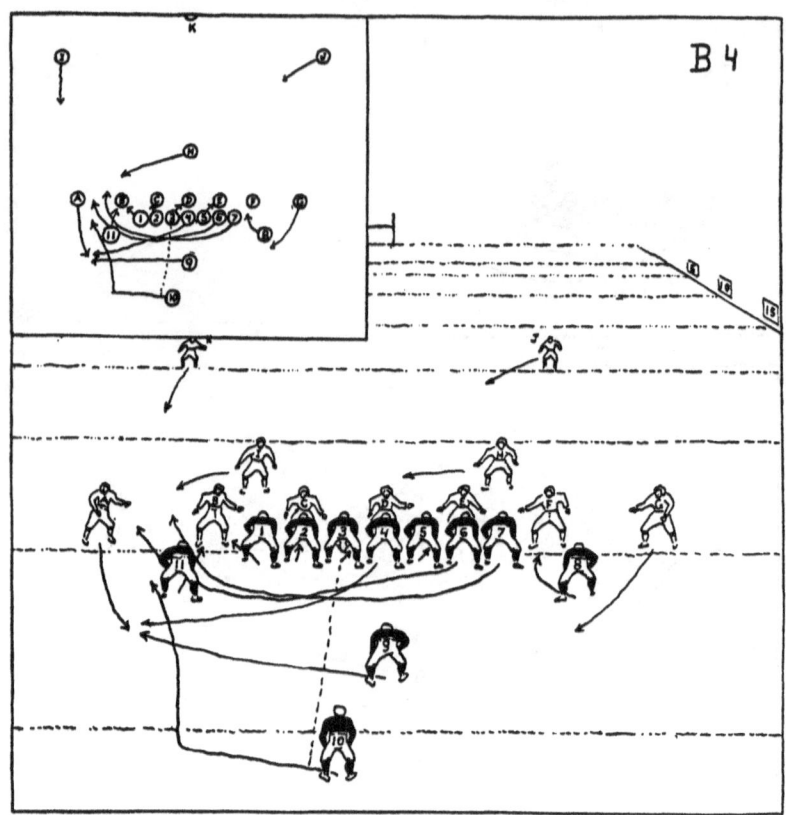

B-4: Off-tackle play to the short side. 4 and 9 block the end out and 6 and 7 swing around outside of defensive tackle, who has been boxed in by 11 and 1. 10 receives the pass from center and moves somewhat slowly to the left as though to circle the end, but he turns sharply just as the end is being taken out and goes inside of the end behind 6 and 7. Here again if a man in motion is used 8 should start ahead of the ball and help 9 on the end while 4 swings around B and blocks off the man backing up the line.

FORMATION B

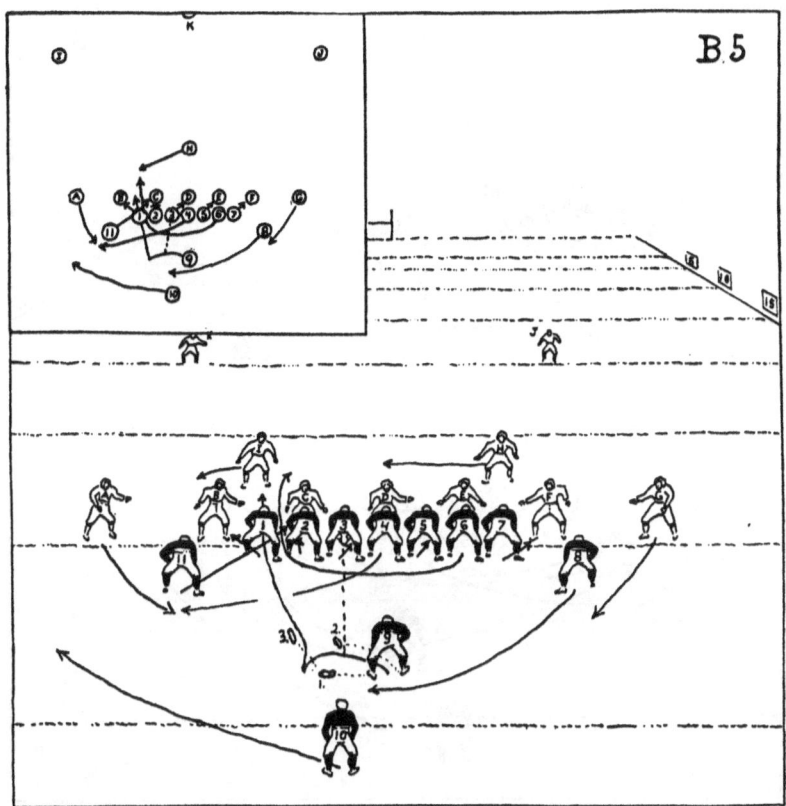

B-5: This is an excellent play, making use of deception but also having plenty of power. 9 receives the ball from center and steps to the left one long step with his left foot, making a half turn by twisting his body and dragging the right foot half way around, at the same time faking the ball to 8. This fake, with 10 running wide and 4 coming out to block the end, makes the play look like a wide one and draws the defensive tackle out. 1 helps him out and 11 cross-blocks, helping 2 box the guard in. 6 swings around and leads the runner through the line. After faking the ball to 8, 9 turns quickly and drives off his left foot into the hole. Having 8 start an instant ahead of the ball helps the play. The footwork of 9 is shown.

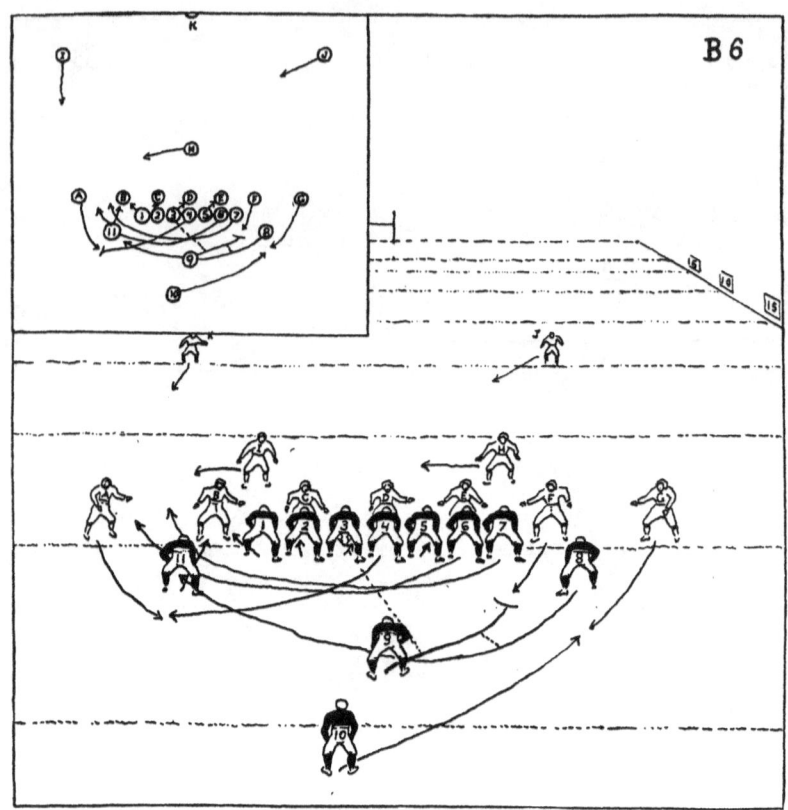

B-6: The famous reverse play to the short side. 9 gets the ball from center and starts off tackle to the right, passing the ball to 8 as they meet and then blocking F. 4 comes out and blocks the end out while 6 and 7 swing around as interference for the runner, 11 and 1 having boxed the tackle in. 2, 3, and 5 block C, D, and E to the right. 10 can run to the right and aid in the deception or he can run to the left as a threat or as an actual receiver of a lateral pass from 8 as shown in B-9 on the reverse to the long side.

FORMATION B

B-7: Fake reverse. 9 gets the ball and takes a long step to the right with his right foot, making a half turn by bringing the left foot a quarter of the way around and twisting the body so that his back is to the scrimmage line while faking the ball to 8. Then he turns back and drives off the right foot into the opening inside of F. 7 drives F out while 6 boxes E in. 4 swings out and carries the end out while 2 comes around and leads 9 through the line. 10 runs wide to the right. The drawing shows the footwork of 9.

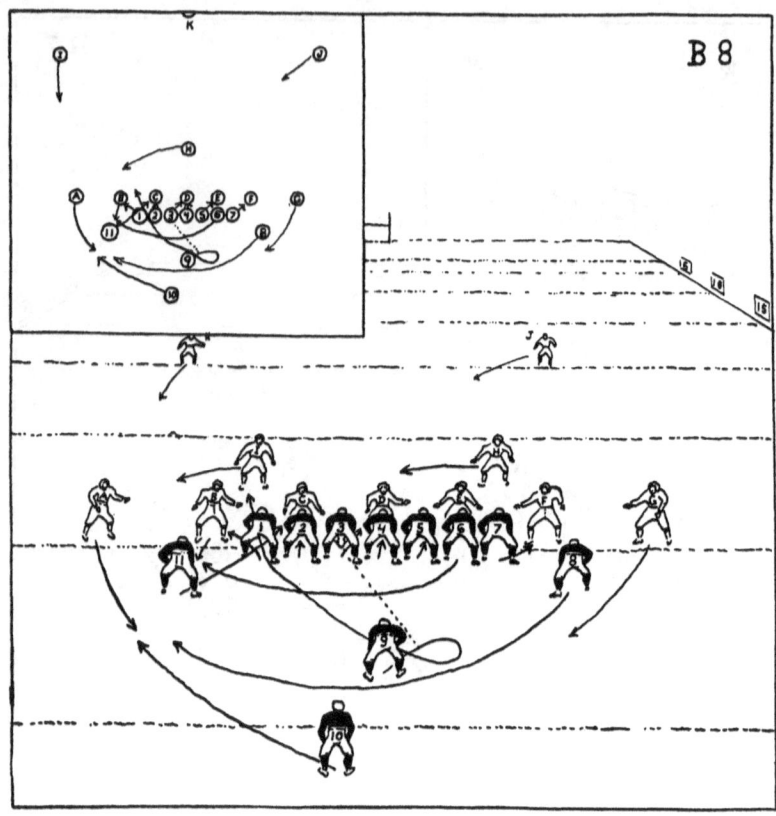

B-8: Fake reverse spin-play. 9 steps toward 8 and fakes to give him the ball for a wide run, but he retains the ball, makes a complete turn while faking, and then shoots inside of defensive tackle who is drawn out by the fake and pushed out by 1. 11 cross-blocks, assisting 2 to drive C in. 6 comes around close to the line and helps carry B out, also aiding in the fake. 10 helps the fake further by running to the left.

FORMATION B

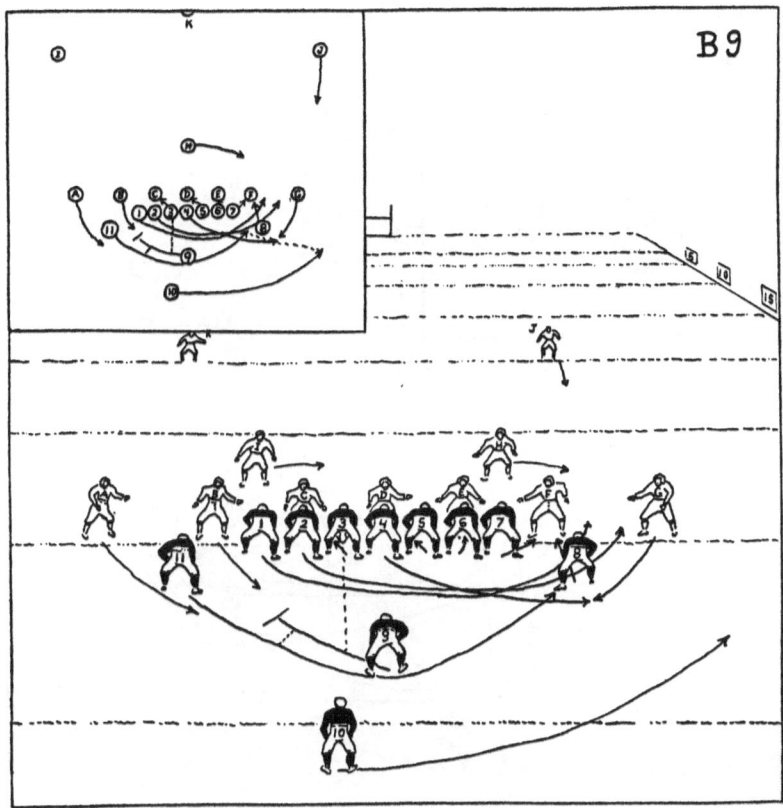

B-9: Reverse to long side and optional lateral pass. 4 comes out and blocks the end out. 1 and 2 come around outside of defensive tackle as interference. 8 and 7 box the tackle in. 9 receives the ball, starts off tackle to the left, and hands the ball to 11 as they meet. 11 turns inside of defensive end and threatens or actually makes a lateral pass to 10, who runs out wide. 6, 5, and 3 block E, D, and C to the left.

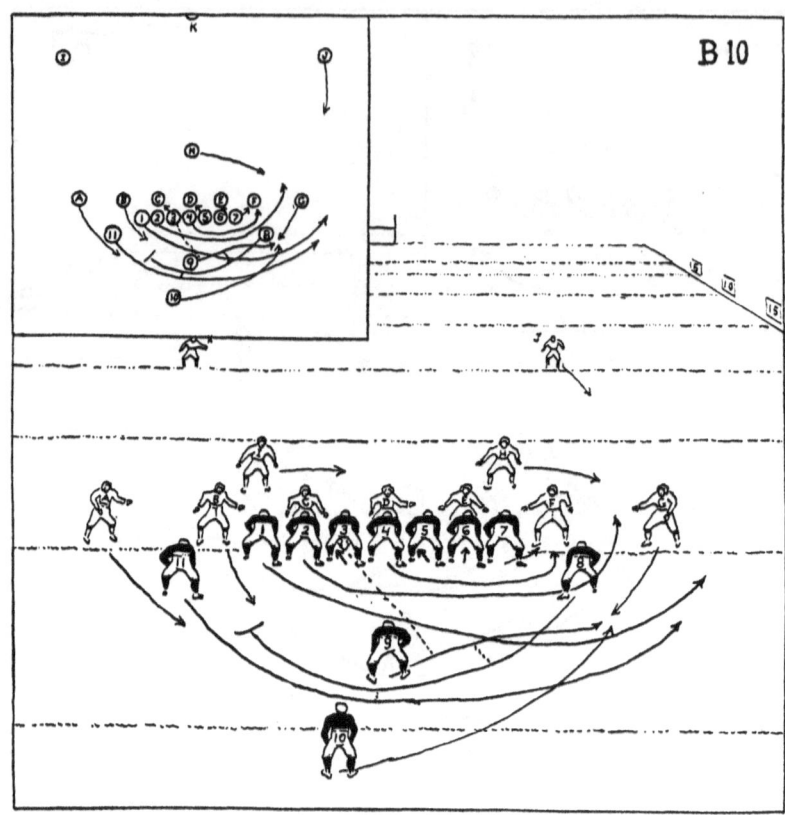

B-10: Triple pass around end, also called the double reverse. 9 starts with the ball, a little wider than in the reverse play B-6, hands the ball to 8 as they meet, and then blocks G. 8 hands the ball to 11 as they meet. 11 has swung well back, and getting the ball from 8 he swings around G with 1 as an interferer. 10 swings to the right and assists in boxing G in. 4 comes around and helps 7 to box F in, and 2 swings outside of F to block off H. 3, 5, and 6 block C, D, and E to the left. Everyone starts with the snap of the ball. 1 is right behind 9 as 9 passes the ball to 8; he then swings outside of 9 and interferes for 10.

FORMATION B

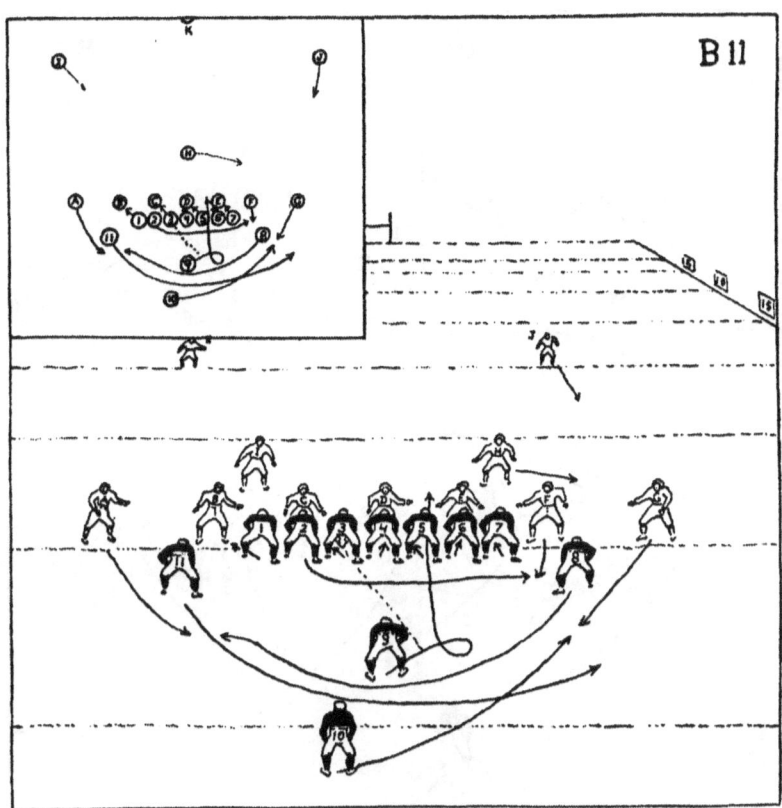

B-11: Spin-play straight ahead with fake double reverse. 9 steps to the right and fakes the ball to 8 and 11 while quickly making a complete turn. He then shoots straight into the line between D and E. 10 blocks G. 2 comes around close to his line and drives F out. 4 and 5 double-team D to the left and 6 and 7 take care of E. Both 8 and 11 should make good fakes to take the ball from 9.

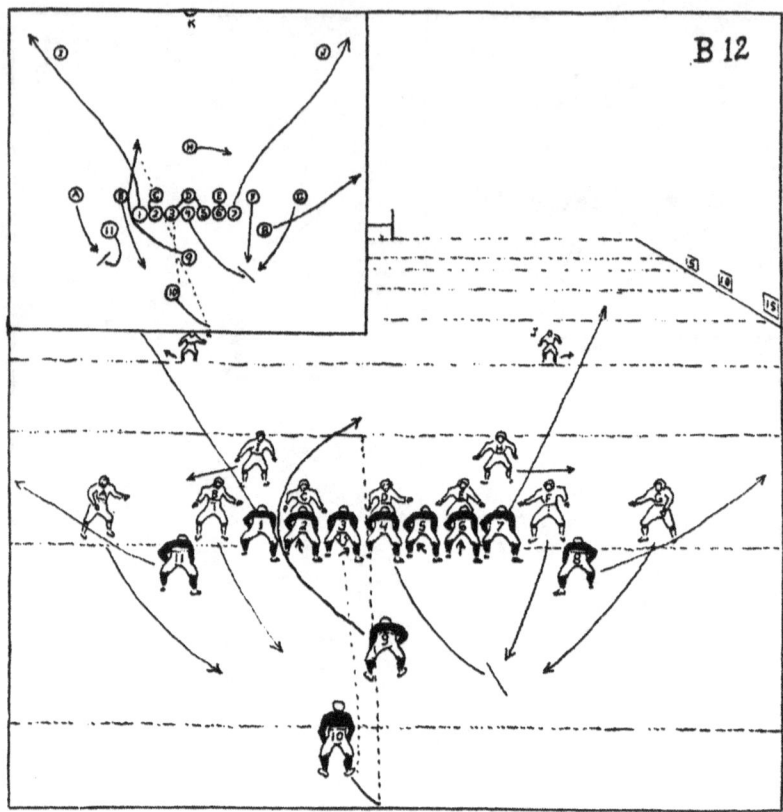

B-12: A very effective short forward pass. The ends 1 and 7 run wide and deep as decoys. 8 runs wide and flat, and against a box defense or a six-man line with center out 11 runs out flat to the left. Against a diamond defense he either blocks A or comes back to the right to help 4 protect the passer. 9 goes through the line outside of C, turns to the right, and takes the pass from 10, who has backed to the rear and a little to the right. Against a diamond defense 9 takes the pass farther to the left so as better to avoid H. 9 must be careful not to run into opponents coming through to hurry the pass.

FORMATION B

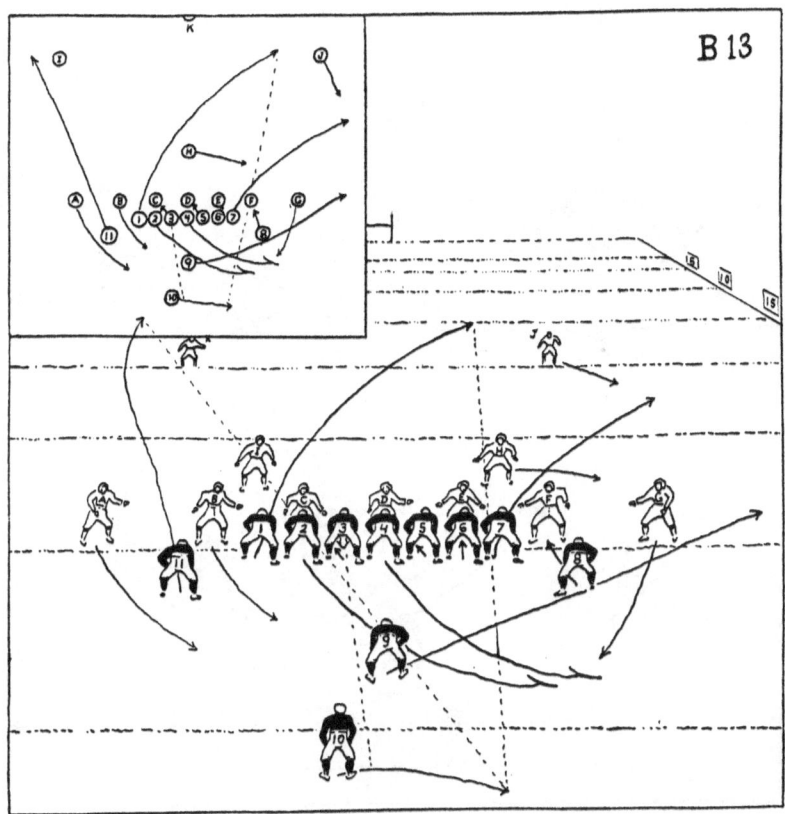

B 13

B-13: A very good long pass. 7 runs out wide to draw J up. 9 runs out flat. 11 runs down deep to the left. 1 runs down the field, swinging in, in back of J and taking the pass from 10, who runs to the right bluffing a flat pass to 9 and then shooting a long one to 1. 2 and 4 come back to protect the passer and 8 stops F.

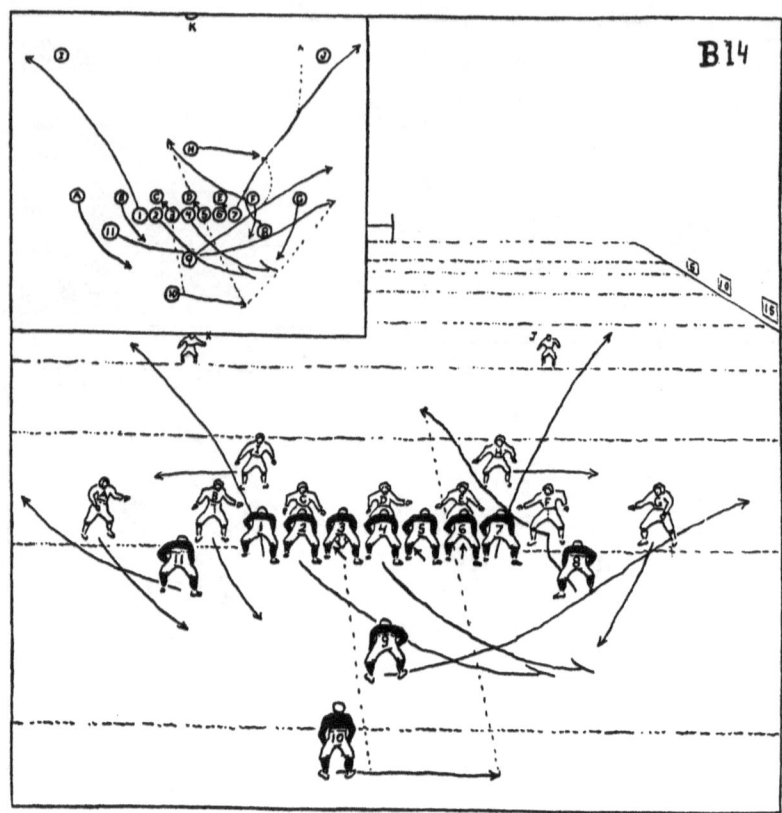

B-14: A good medium-distance pass. 1 and 7 run deep and wide. Against a box defense or where the center is playing out of the line 11 and 9 run out flat on their side, but against a diamond defense 11 comes around to the right and flat while 9 runs a little deeper. 8 first blocks the tackle and then sneaks five or six yards straight over center and takes the pass from 10, who runs to the right and bluffs a pass to 9. Against a diamond defense a good pass can also be made to 11, in which case 9 and 7 should vary their play as shown by the dotted lines in the upper diagram, and 10 should bluff to 8.

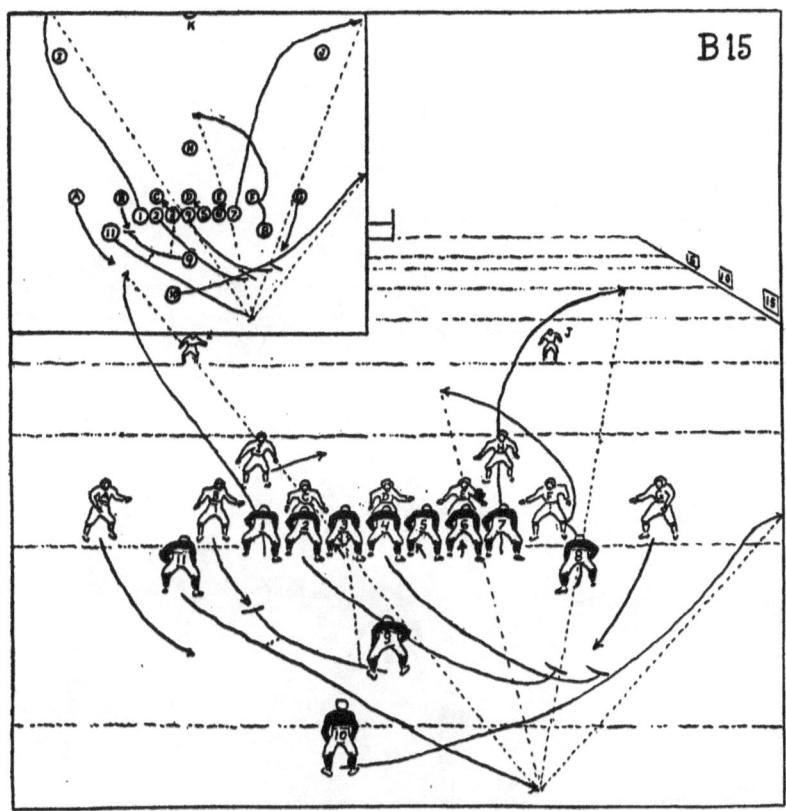

B-15: Four good passes are here shown, in each of which all the eligible receivers run the same way. 9 carries the ball to 11 as in the reverse play, but he runs wider so that 11 can swing well back. 9 blocks B after handing the ball to 11, and 2 and 4 swing well back to protect the passer. 8 blocks F and then goes down the center. The other receivers run as shown. I have found it best to have one signal for a pass to either 7 or 10 and another signal for an optional pass to either 1 or 8.

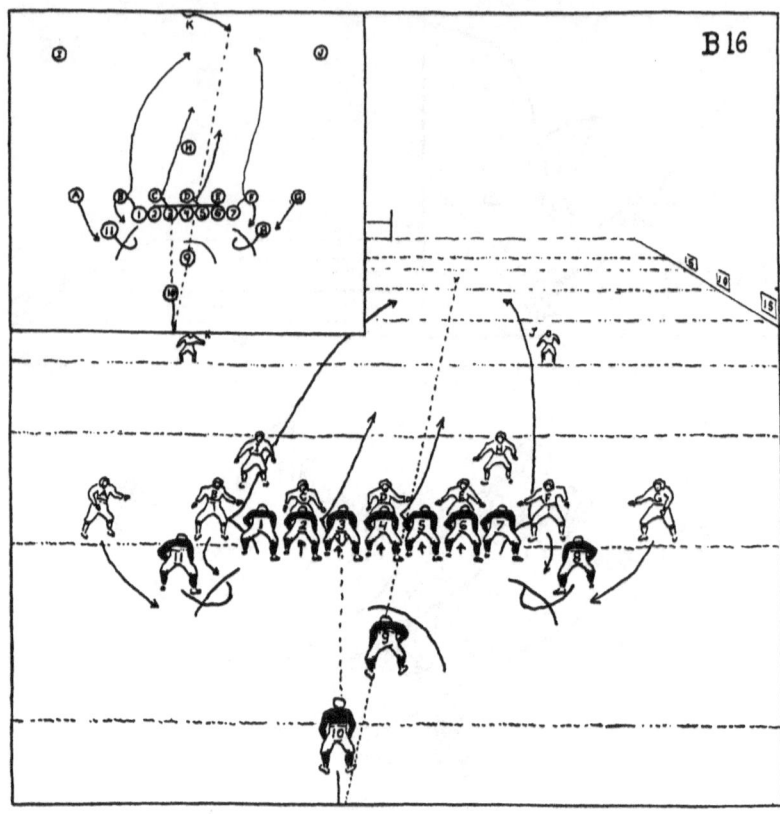

B-16: Quick punt from "B" formation. 10 backs up as the ball is being passed to him for the kick, which should be gotten off quickly. The ends, 1 and 7, push the tackles out before starting down the field, using a quick shoulder block. 11 and 8 step back and toward the center and block either the tackles or ends, whichever looks the most dangerous. 9 looks first to see that no one is coming through the line, and if not he blocks to the right if 10 is a right-footed kicker. The five center men block shoulder to shoulder, 5 helping on D and then going down the field and 3 helping on C and then going down. This is an excellent play to use as a surprise kick against a box defense or where the safety man is playing close up on first, second, or third down.

PUNT FORMATION

This is a good formation for punting, passing, and rushing the ball. It is slightly different from the standard punt formation in that one of the backs is stationed outside of the defensive tackle and close to the line on the right, where he is of more value in running and forward-pass plays, and is also in a position to block the tackle and help protect the kicker on punts.

In this formation the ends should be out about three yards from their tackles and in a position from which they can box the tackles in on wide runs to their side. They should play in the same position whether the play is to be a run, a punt, or a pass. Two backs are stationed about four yards behind the line and directly behind the openings between their guards and tackles. The rear man is ten yards back of the ball.

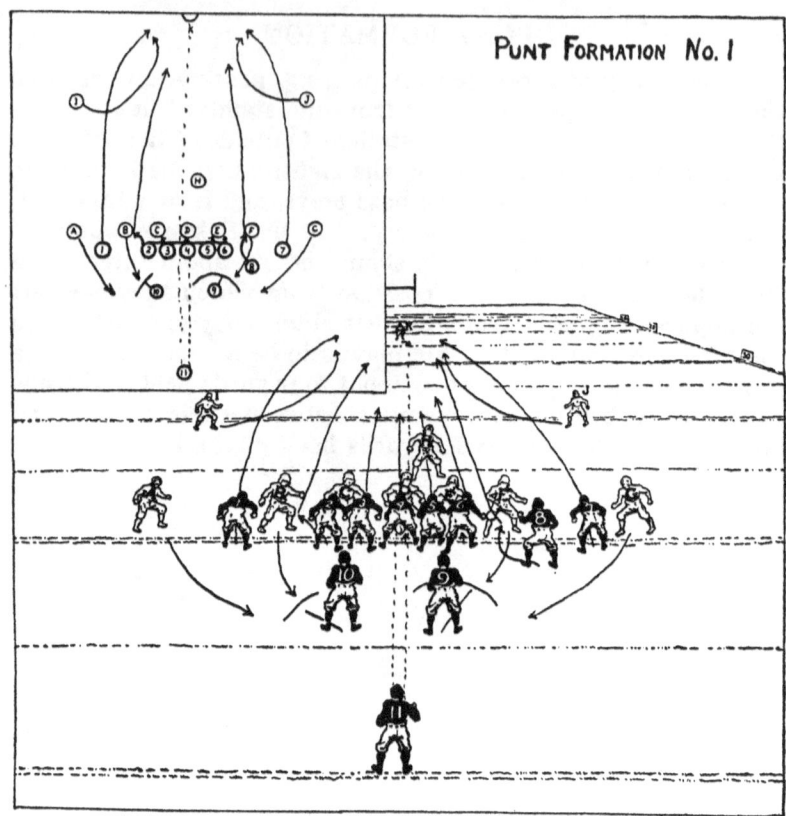

P-1: The punt. The ends, 1 and 7, should go down fast without blocking unless A and G come in very close, in which case they shoulder the ends out as they start down the field, especially on fourth down when the opponents know a punt is coming. 8 blocks F, forcing him to go on the outside, and then goes down the field. The five center men block shoulder to shoulder, except that 2 can usually shoulder his man, B, out and then go down the field. 10 blocks to the left, taking either B or A, whichever seems to be most dangerous. 9 blocks to the right in the same way, first seeing that no one is coming through center. 11 must be back at least ten yards unless he is an exceptionally fast punter. On fourth down or when kicking near his own goal he should be back more than ten yards.

PUNT FORMATION

P-2: Tandem buck through center. Two-on-one against the opponents between whom the play is made, with 10 leading 9 through and blocking off the man backing up the line. Against a seven-man line the same play can be made to go between D and E, with 10 taking the ball and 9 leading him through. Against a six-man line the center, 4, can go through and block off D, as shown in the upper diagram.

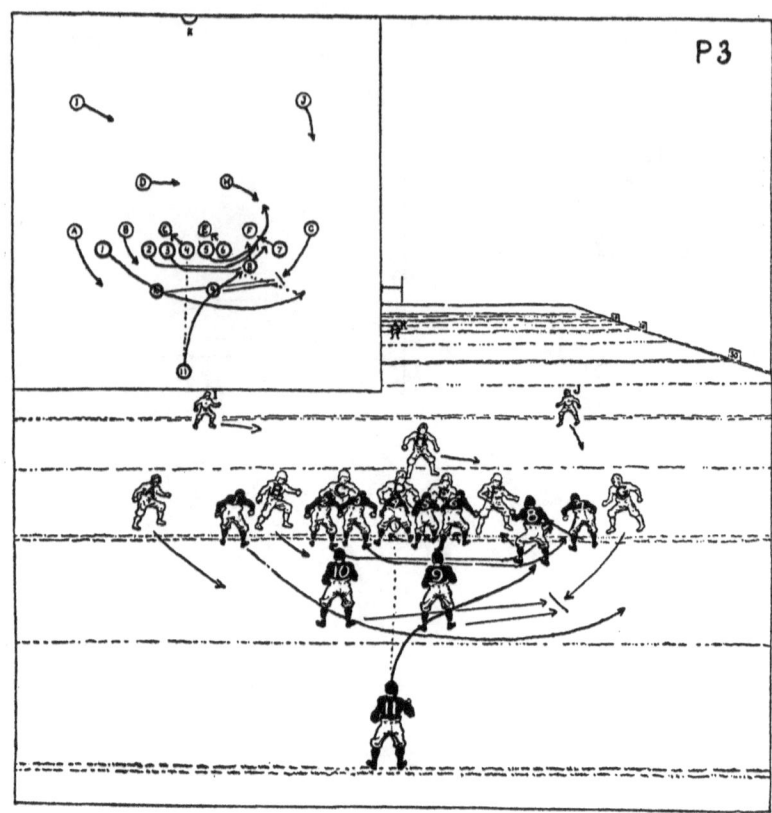

P-3: Off-tackle play to the right with a lateral pass, threatened or executed. 7 and 8 box the tackle in. 4, 5, and 6 block C, D, and E to the left. 2 and 3 swing around F for interference, while 10 and 9 drive the end out. 11 starts directly forward on the snap of the ball and then veers off to the right behind 2 and 3. 1 swings well back and wide, and 11 can toss him a lateral pass or can continue with the ball. Against a six-man line 5 can swing around and take H, as shown in the upper diagram.

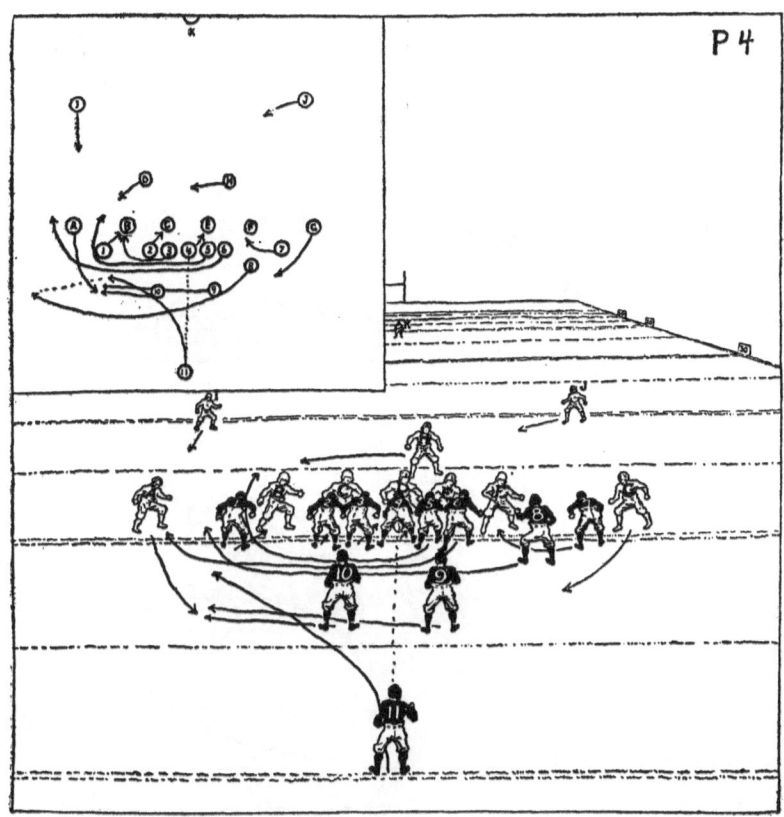

P-4: Off-tackle play to the left. 1 boxes B in. Against a seven-man line 2, 3, and 4 block C, D, and E to the right. Against a six-man line 3 comes out and helps 1 on B. 5 and 6 come around outside of B for interference and 8 can do the same, unless the play is played as in the upper diagram when he swings back and wide to be in a position to receive a lateral pass. The play can be run either way. 11 starts directly forward, getting the ball from center and then turning to the left behind 5 and 6. 9 and 10 block the end out.

P-5: Off-tackle play, or lateral pass. 8 and 7 box the tackle in and 4 and 6 block D and E to the left—or C and E if against a six-man line. 5 comes around F and blocks off H. 2 and 3 swing a little wider as interference for the runner, 10, who starts wide and swings in behind 2 and 3 or makes a lateral pass to 11. 9 blocks the end out. 1 cuts off B and goes through for secondary. 11 swings wide to be in a position to receive a lateral pass or to draw G out.

PUNT FORMATION

P-6: Reverse play to left with lateral pass or lateral pass threat. Against a six-man line 3 can come out and help 1 on the tackle, but against a seven-man line 2, 3, and 4 block C, D, and E to the left. 5 and 6 come around outside of B for interference and 10 blocks the end out. 9 starts at F with the ball, handing it to 8, who swings around behind 5 and 6, making a lateral pass to 11 if A comes in sharply or if 1 is unable to box B.

180 FOOTBALL FOR COACHES AND PLAYERS

P-7: On this play 1 plays rather close to his tackle and 8 plays fairly close to 6 to make it certain that F will be compelled to charge outside of him. 9 receives the ball from 4 and turns and fakes the ball to 11 and also to 1. In these fakes 9 makes a complete turn and no time should be wasted by being too deliberate in faking. The threat of 1 and 11 running wide should cause F to charge wide. 3 leaves his position and pushes F out as he comes in. 8 cross-blocks E. 10 starts slowly and leads 9 through the line just outside of E. Against a six-man line 6 blocks the tackle, F, out.

Try this and the succeeding play and use the one which the team executes the more cleverly and which gets the best results.

PUNT FORMATION

P-8: Fake double pass. 9 receives the ball from center and pivots on his left foot without taking a step with that foot, but bringing the right foot part way around and turning the body so that the ball is well concealed from the line while making the fake to 10. 9 then drives off the left foot, just outside of E. F should be drawn wide by the fake and 5 helps him along. 8 cross-blocks E, helping 6. 7 goes through and takes J, or if G is playing in close he had better block him out. 11 swings wide.

Try this play also with 9 turning to the right and spinning around while faking, as in the preceding play, P-7, and see which method works best.

P-9: Here are two good long passes, and also a good flat pass against a diamond defense. The latter pass is not so good against a box or a six-man-line defense. 1 and 7 run deep and inside the defensive backs and then swing toward the side lines. 9 runs out flat to the right. 8, if the pass is to be made to him, blocks H. 10 runs out to the left not quite so flat as 9. When the pass is to be made to 7, 9 runs a little deeper so as to attract the attention of J. On the long passes to either 7 or 1, 8 should block F in order to give the passer more time. Both guards (3 and 5) swing back to protect the passer, who runs to the right while fixing the ball in his hands.

PUNT FORMATION

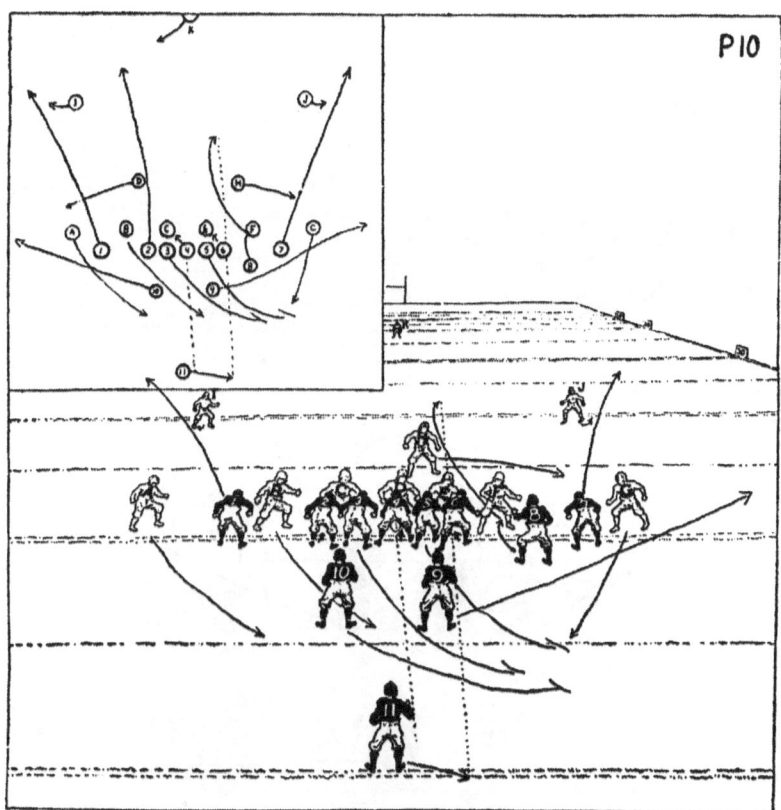

P-10: A very effective medium-length pass. 7 and 1 run deep and outside the defensive halfbacks to draw the latter out. 9 runs out flat to the right. Against a six-man line or a box defense 10 should run out flat to the left, but when only one man is backing up the line he should come back with 3 and 5 to protect the passer. 8 first blocks the tackle so as to avoid suspicion and then sneaks about seven to ten yards beyond the center of the scrimmage line and receives the pass from 11, who steps to the right and first makes believe he is going to pass to 9.

P-11: An excellent flat pass to the left. 10, 1, and 7 all run deep and to the right while 9 runs out flat to the right. 8 works his way carefully to the left, running close to his line and being careful not to bump into anyone coming through. 11 steps to the right, fakes a pass to 9, and then throws it to 8 just over the scrimmage line. 3 comes back to protect the passer but 5 stays in so as not to collide with 8. 2 and 4 first block and then pull over as shown, so as to make the play safe in case the pass is intercepted.

PUNT FORMATION

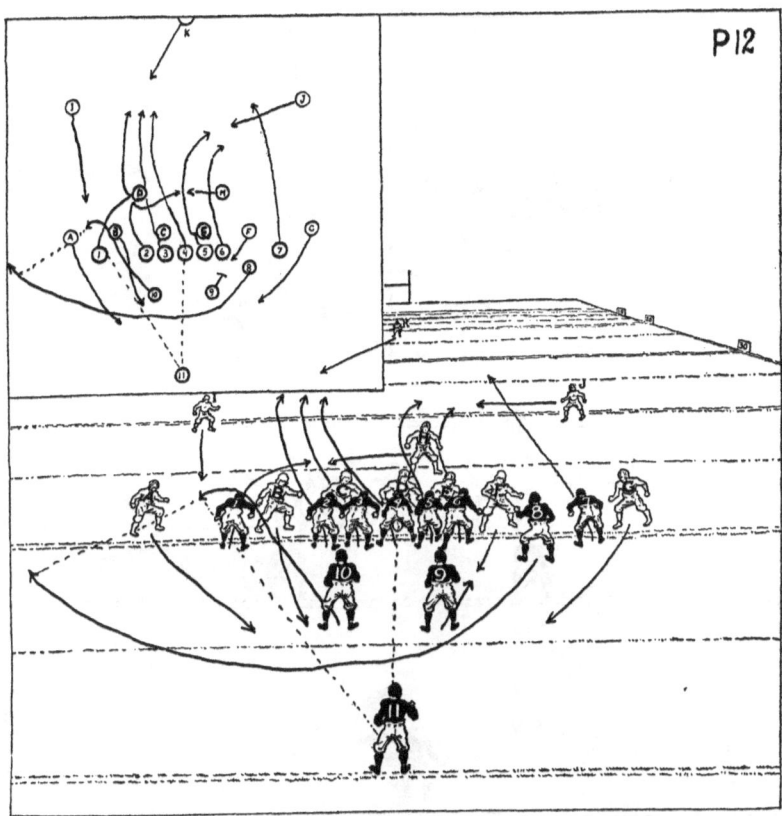

P-12: This is a touchdown play, making use of a forward and then a lateral pass, and it has actually scored several touchdowns against superior teams. It works best against a diamond defense. 11 bluffs a punt and then tosses the ball to 10, who gets into position on the left about two or three yards beyond the scrimmage line and facing 11 or toward the side line. As he catches the pass I will come up to tackle him just as he is making a lateral pass to 8, who has swung around wide. This gives a clear field with the exception of the safety man, who should be blocked off by the linemen running down the field. 1 cuts off H, or the back on his side if two men are backing up the line. 11 has to make an overhand lob pass over the heads of A and B, who will be charging in.

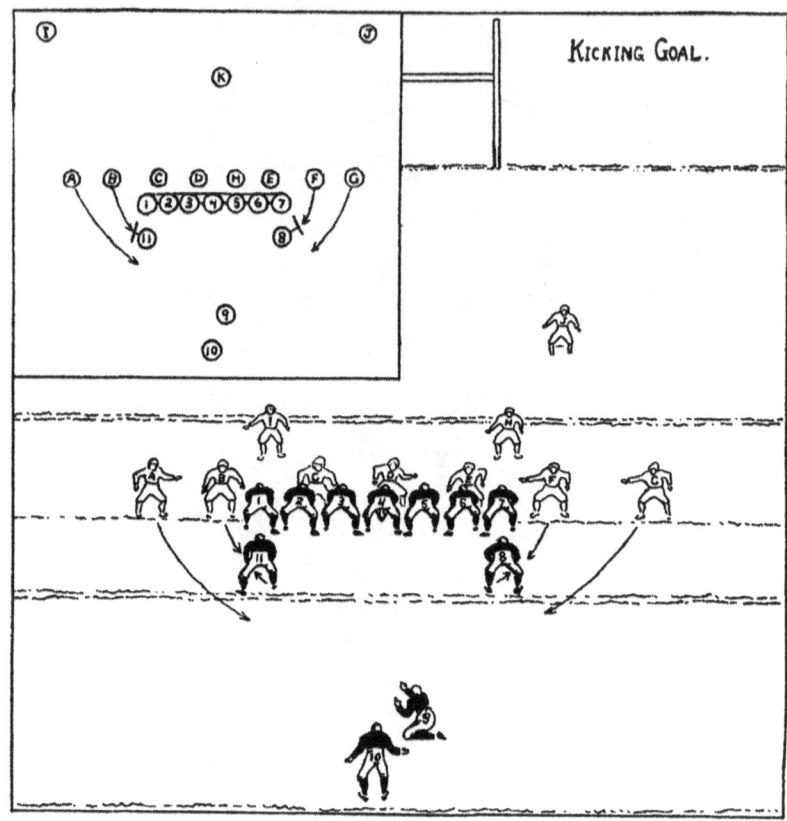

Kicking Goal: The line is regular and should play close together, shoulder to shoulder. 11 and 8 are directly behind their ends, close up and facing somewhat outward. They must prevent B and F from getting inside of them, being sure to block them out as they charge in. 9, who holds the ball for a place-kick, is not back more than six yards. If the ball is kicked from a point more than six yards back the defensive ends may be able to get in front of it, but at six yards they cannot get around 8 and 11, who are blocking F and B, and over in front of the ball. If using a drop-kick, 9 stands behind 8 and before he blocks G watches to see that no one is breaking through the line. (See chapter on place-kicking, pages 52–56.)

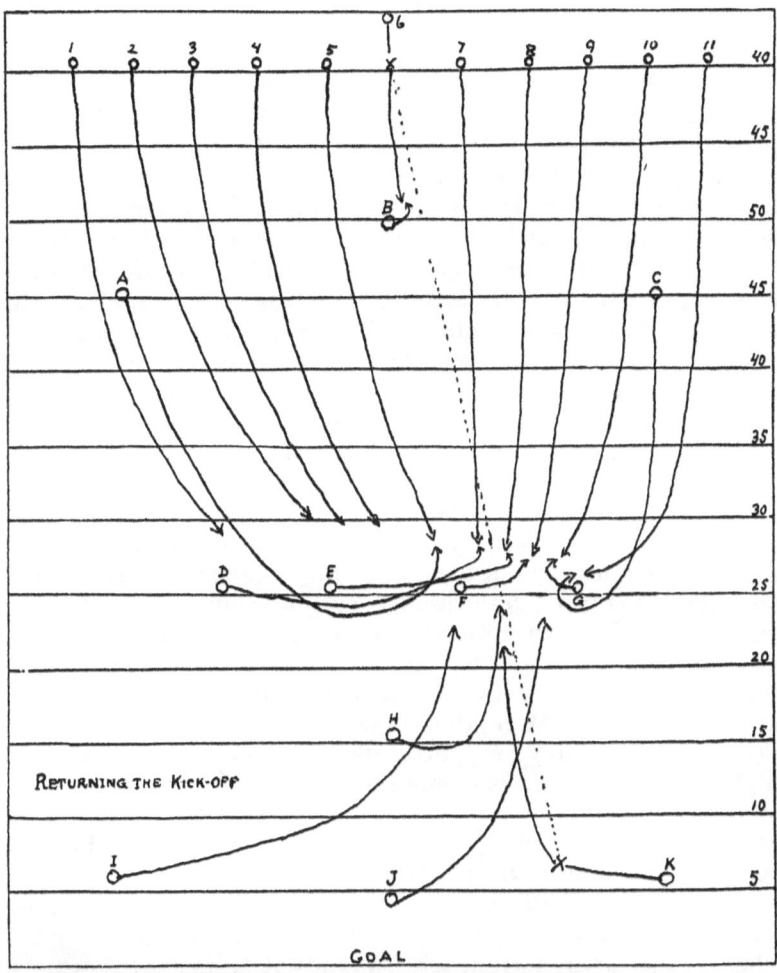

Returning the Kick-off: On this play it is better that the forwards have certain men to block than that they merely form in a group and take whoever gets in their path. On the kick going to the right halfback, K, the players understand that they are going to block off the men on the right. If the ball goes to the left half, I, they will block the men on the left; and if the ball goes to J they will block the six center men, B always taking the kicker. Thus the six opponents who have the shortest distance to run are blocked individually, and the ball-carrier has three general interferers.

D, E, F, and G simply move over so as to be in front of their assignments. A, D, and E block their opponents to the left, and F, G, and C block their men to the right, thus leaving an opening through the center of these six forwards.

DEFENSE

Football is a game in which the rules are so made as to equalize the offense and defense. There is a defense to every play that can be devised, providing the defensive team is equal in strength and skill to the opposing team. If that were not true there would nearly always be plenty of scoring by both teams in games in which opponents are rather evenly matched; but in a perfectly played game, theoretically only the winning team should score. The records show that in the majority of games the losers score nothing. It is only when such mistakes as blocked kicks, fumbles, intercepted passes, missed tackles, etc., are made, or when both teams have developed a better offense than they have a defense, that there is scoring by both teams. There is much more scoring by both teams in the games now than there was years ago, when possession of the ball was more important and a closer and more conservative style of play was in vogue. Teams take many more chances under the rules as they now stand, the ball changes hands oftener, a more open game is played, and fumbles and misplays are much more common than they were in the old days. However, the forward pass no doubt more than any other play is responsible for increased scoring by the losing team. In a forward-passing attack the size and strength of opponents do not cut much figure because in this play very little physical contact between man and man is involved. It is more a case of speed and cleverness, so that the team which is lighter and weaker physically is not severely handicapped against a more powerful team when the former is playing a passing game. Offensive football requires a great deal more drill and practice than defensive play because so many plays and signals have to be learned, but defensive play is fully as important and should not be neglected.

A good defense requires good tacklers, good charging in the line, and alertness of a high order. The players must be so placed that they are in favorable positions for defending against both running plays and forward passes, and every player should have certain well-defined duties to perform. A good defense should also be elastic enough to be varied to meet the type of play which is most likely to be used. It stands to reason that when the opponents have but a yard or two to go for a first down a power play may logically be expected, and at such a time there would be no sense in the line playing wide and the backs well back, as they should play when the offensive team has a long distance to go for a first down. In the latter case the defense to power plays through the line can be weakened in order to strengthen the defense to forward passes, because if power plays should be used the defense probably is never so weakened that it will not be able to keep such plays from gaining enough to attain the desired end. In other words, a short gain may be conceded the offensive team in a case like that.

I have seen coaches place their defensive players in certain positions with reference to the ball and insist that they maintain those positions regardless of the down and distance to gain. This is a brainless method, since it allows of no variation to meet the many changing conditions which are bound to arise during a game, and does not cultivate nor promote such alertness and generalship as are necessary for a good defense.

There are several system of both line and backfield defense. These have been discussed to some extent in the chapters dealing with the playing of individual positions. Some coaches teach a standing line defense and others insist that their linemen shall be low and on all fours and shall charge through on every play. Both methods are good for certain conditions, and if an elastic and varied defense is taught both methods should be used—the standing line against punt and open formations and against any formation when there is a long distance to be gained, and the low, hard-charging line against close formations at all times except when the distance that has to be gained is so great that a line play is not feared.

Ends are coached differently by different coaches, some preferring that their wing men play a cautious game and try to sift through the interference to tackle the runner or drive him in toward his tackle, while others coach their ends to rush in sharply, their primary duty being to smash up the plays, leaving much of the tackling to be done by the other players. Both systems are good provided the right system of defense is used by the other players to fit in with the two types of end play. If the cautious style is used the tackles should play the smashing type of tackle play and the halfbacks need not play so wide, because there is little danger of players getting around the ends. If the smashing type of end play is used the tackles should play a little more cautiously, and the halfbacks should play a little wider and closer up so that they are in a favorable position for rushing up and tackling runners who succeed in getting around the ends.

Some coaches use a six-man line with the center playing back and backing up the line with the fullback. This is a stronger method of play than the seven-man line to stop open plays such as end runs and forward passes, but it is not so good for defending against power plays. Here again is a great opportunity for the use of headwork by the defense, and both methods should be taught and the team instructed to use the method best suited to the down and distance to be gained, the center dropping back to strengthen the secondary defense when an open play or a pass is likely and remaining in the line when a power play, such as a line buck or off-tackle play, is the logical thing. If the center plays out of the line the tackles and guards should move in somewhat, so that the spaces in the line between the four center players are about equal.

There are two separate and distinct styles of secondary or backfield defense, commonly called the box defense and the diamond defense. The latter style was standard for many years, one man playing close behind his line, two men playing almost directly back of their ends and from seven to ten yards to the rear, and the fourth man, usually designated as the safety man, from twenty to thirty yards directly back of the ball.

The box defense was originated and has been developed most highly by Gil Dobie, head coach at Cornell, who has had signal success with it. There have been many converts to this system, which provides for two men backing up the line rather close up and about behind the tackles, with the other two backs twelve to fifteen yards back and to either side. In this system there is no safety man, and punts, especially quick ones, are often kicked over the heads of the backs. This style, however, provides a better defense to running plays and probably also to forward passes, and these advantages are figured to more than make up for the weakness in defending against quick kicks. Many teams use a combination of these two systems, using the diamond defense in the opponent's territory and in the center of the field, and the box defense in their own territory. This is a very good plan.

Against a team using the shifting style of attack, such as the Notre Dame or the so-called Minnesota shift, the proper defense requires that the defensive players shift with the offensive team, and in order to do this quickly and easily the linemen should be on their feet rather than down low with their hands on the ground. The shift should be made quickly, and after shifting the linemen can come to the crouching stance if the situation demands a low, hard charge. In shifting to meet a shift attack the defensive team will do well to move a little farther than the offensive team, because in about nine plays out of ten the play will go to the side toward which the shift is made, and a defensive team whose players are taught to shift more than the offensive team does will usually hold a shifting team at a great disadvantage.

Against any one-sided formation the defense should get in front of the opposing team, no matter where the ball is, and the defensive team should aim to have a little more strength on the long side of the ball than the offensive team has, because the weak-side plays of most teams are not strong and are little used.

Defense to Forward Passes

There are three types or systems of defense to forward passing. These are the zone defense, the man-to-man defense, and a modified form of man-to-man defense. In the zone defense the players playing back of the line of scrimmage, commonly called the secondary defensive players, are so stationed that they can knock down or intercept any pass which comes into their territory or zone. These men do not spot an opponent and follow him wherever he goes, but instead they play the ball and move about in their zone, covering any eligible pass receiver who comes into it. In the man-to-man defense each player of the secondary defense must select a certain eligible pass receiver and cover him wherever he may go. Each man is responsible for the man he is to cover rather than for any certain territory, as he is in the zone defense. In the modified man-to-man defense the secondary defense men cover certain men to the point where the men they are covering pass out of their zone and another man is coming into it, in which case he may leave the covering of the first man to a team-mate and himself cover the man who has deployed into his territory and appears to be more likely to receive the pass.

There appears to be a great difference of opinion as to which is the best of these three defenses, some of the best coaches favoring and using the first method, other equally experienced and successful mentors using the second, and still others banking on the third system. It is possible that any one of them is good provided it is properly executed by alert players properly coached in the system chosen. I believe that most coaches use the man-to-man defense in preference to the others, but in my judgment there are several reasons why the zone system is preferable. In the first place the zone defense is easier on the players and easier to execute. It does not require that men executing it run all over the field trying to cover certain men: all the zone defense demands is that the players stationed in the different zones be not decoyed out of position. They simply stay where they are when a pass is expected, each moving about in his zone only enough to cover any eligible receiver coming into it, and playing the ball. There are four secondary defense men except when the center adds a fifth by playing out of the line, and these four or five men, if they simply remain stationary in their tracks until the pass is made, can probably knock down or intercept nine-tenths of the passes that are made. Against this defense few passes are made except when some one or more of these men are fooled into believing the play is going to be a run instead of a pass or are cleverly decoyed out of their zones.

In the man-to-man defense the man rather than the ball is played and the player whose duty it is to cover a certain man may have to run over to the other side of the field to follow his man, paying no attention to his zone. The offensive ends may cross to opposite sides of the field or one of them may run behind his own line over to the other side, and it would seem that fast receivers getting the start on opponents would stand a better chance of getting to the ball. This defense seems to involve unnecessary effort and it demands a speed not required in the zone defense, and unless the center is out of the line there are but four defensive backs to cover five eligible receivers.

The modified defense requires much practice, great team

work, and quick thinking in turning over to a team-mate at the right time the responsibility of covering a certain man. The system is dangerous in that it may result in mistakes which are often disastrous.

The covering of zones or of men by the backfield players is but a part of a good forward-pass defense. All coaches agree that an important factor in a good pass defense is fast rushing of the passer, and at least two and sometimes all of the linemen are coached to get to the passer as quickly as possible so that he has little time to pick out his man or to hesitate until the receiver is uncovered. If the passer is hurried in his throw he is also less accurate in his passing, and many a pass is spoiled by the quickness with which the opposing ends or tackles get to the passer and either block the throw or tackle the man before he can get rid of the ball.

GENERALSHIP

Under this head it is intended to treat not only of the generalship with which an important game should be handled, but also of the intelligent management of the whole season's campaign. Much of this chapter is taken almost verbatim from my former book on football published in 1912, because football strategy has changed very little since that time.

The Schedule

The schedule is generally arranged with the idea of providing the team with practice games early in the season, the games increasing in importance as the season progresses and leading up to one or two final championship games which are made the climax of the season, and for which nearly every other game is considered as a means of development and preparation.

The strongest teams as a rule try to arrange their schedules so that the games will be comparatively easy at the start, growing harder as the season advances, but with the idea always in mind of reaching the final championship game or games without defeat. The weaker teams very often arrange their early games with stronger teams out of their class, realizing that they are almost sure to be beaten, but believing that the games will give the players practice and experience which will aid them later in the season in their championship games with teams in their own class.

Occasionally a supposedly minor team will be blessed with unusually good material which will get together early and by developing quickly will try to surprise a so-called "big" team with which they have scheduled an early practice game. If the minor team happens to win such a game, it gives the players some temporary glory and notoriety, but usually results in disaster before the end of the season by reason of the overconfidence or "swelled head" engendered by the victory and of overtraining resulting from getting into topnotch condition too soon. While it is a laudable thing for every team to desire to win all the games possible, still the success of the season will usually be greater if the early games are considered as practice games pure and simple, with no special preparation made for them. The games later in the season are usually the ones upon which the standing of the team or the success of the season is based, and these should be the contests to be borne in mind during the season and gradually worked up to. In doing this, the other games should not be overlooked by any means, nor played without putting forth every effort and making such careful preparations as will not interfere with the steady and gradual development of the team.

Some schedules are arranged in such a manner that a very important game has to be played in the middle of the season and another at the end. With such a schedule, the team is usually developed rather early and put in prime condition for the mid-season game, after which it is easily handled for a week or two, and then developed for the second or final climax. A team which has a schedule arranged in this manner will very seldom play in topnotch form in both of these games, and unless it is unusually strong is almost sure to be beaten in one of them. With a schedule like this, it will prove to be good generalship to regard the final game as the most important, and not have the team at the top of its form for the midseason contest. It will be wise to follow both suggestions, because if the midseason game should be won without being in peak form, but with the idea that it was of more importance than the final contest, overconfidence and lack of interest would then ruin the team's chances in the latter game.

About the poorest schedule a team can have is one in which the most important game comes about the middle of the season, which closes with games of minor importance. A team with such an arrangement of games may do well in the early season and in its important game, but is almost sure to deteriorate and spoil its reputation in the latter part of the season by reason of overconfidence and lack of interest and enthusiasm.

No matter how the schedule is arranged, it should be the aim of every team to make gradual and steady improvement as the season progresses. If defeats come, everything possible should be done to keep the players from becoming disheartened, and the defects in the team's play which caused the defeats should be pointed out to the players and corrected. No schedule should be arranged which will necessitate playing more than half the games with teams known to be stronger than the team for which it is arranged, because nothing will so dishearten the players as several successive defeats. One or two defeats in early or mid-season usually aid in developing a team, because they bring out weak points and keep the players in a receptive mood for coaching. It is just as great a mistake to arrange too easy a schedule as it is too hard a one. If the practice games leading to the final game or games are all with teams of a minor class and are easily won, the championship games will be reached without having had a chance to test properly the players or the plays. Some players will appear to excellent advantage in the minor games, but will be found wanting when up against strong opponents; and many plays which work well against weaker teams will be found worthless in games where the teams are evenly matched. Therefore every team should have some games with worthy opponents before the championship games are reached, in order that the faint-hearted or easily rattled players and the unsuccessful plays may be weeded out.

The Material

Good judgment or generalship should be exercised in handling the material and in placing the players in the positions for which they are best fitted. No matter how good the backs may be they cannot accomplish much behind a weak line, while mediocre backs will be able to get good results behind a strong line; therefore it is of first importance so to arrange the players as to provide a strong line. As a rule it will be found that the inexperienced candidates, provided they have sufficient weight, will be able to do better work as guards or at center than in any other position, because experience and knowledge of the game are not so necessary for the three center men. A player who has had considerable experience as a guard can easily learn to play tackle, and as a rule a player who has learned to play tackle can be developed into a good end, provided he has enough speed. So a good rule to follow in arranging the players in the line is to place the inexperienced men in the three center positions and move out the experienced ones, placing those with the greatest experience and most ability at the ends.

In choosing a field general the coach should select the liveliest, coolest, and headiest player among the candidates, in whom the other players have the utmost confidence.

The heaviest of the backfield material should as a rule be placed in the position of fullback, and in selecting all of the backs their defensive ability should be regarded as being just as important as their ability to advance the ball. Every team should have at least two good punters and a field-goal kicker in its makeup, although these need not necessarily be backs.

Left-handed and left-footed players are better suited to positions upon the right side of the line than upon the left.

The man in charge of the handling and the selection of material must be a general, as he has all kinds of temperaments to deal with and will be confronted with many situations which must be handled with tact and diplomacy. He must show no favoritism, and should endeavor by all means to keep the players in good humor, and free from jealousies and ill-feeling toward each other. Harmony should be the watchword of the season, because no combination of individuals working together for a common purpose can secure the best results unless they pull together—an axiom especially true of football teams.

Planning the Campaign

In preparing for all except the early practice games, a study should be made of the systems of offense and defense relied upon by the opponents, so that the players may be instructed as to the best methods of meeting them. The plays may have to be changed slightly from week to week in order to cope with different styles of defense, while the formations and plays relied upon by opposing teams will necessitate changes in the regular system of defense. In the practice games of the week it is a good plan to have the scrub or second team play as nearly as possible the same style of game used by the team which will be met on Saturday.

Having learned how to meet different systems or styles of play as the season progresses, the players will be ready to meet almost any situation in the final games, and will not be rendered helpless by having something new sprung on them.

A special study should be made of the style of game played by the team or teams with whom the championship games are to be played, and the whole season should be centered upon these games. While the other games should be prepared for and played with determination and spirit, they should be regarded as of minor importance, and every effort be put forth to instill in the players the importance of the championship game or games, and an intense desire and determination to fairly overcome their rivals.

The mental attitude of the players toward the opponents or the games plays a very important part in the results of many games. No team will do its best if the players go into a game without a full realization that they will have to put forth their best efforts to win, or are overconfident; and very often under such conditions the unexpected strength and determination of the opponents will so surprise, daze, and demoralize a team that the game results in a disastrous defeat, which might have been avoided if the players had gone into the game with the right spirit.

The Game

During the week preceding a championship game the team should be handled very carefully. If there are any players suffering from injuries they should not engage in any rough exercise, and the practice of the week should be devoted to smoothing up the plays and perfecting the team work.

If the game is to be played away from home, but within a two or three hours' ride, the trip will interfere less with the players if it is taken on the morning of the day of the game than it will if taken the day before, because the players will rest better in their own beds and will not be so affected by nervous excitement as they would be in a strange place, near the scene of the coming struggle. When the game is to be played more than a hundred miles from home, the trip should be made the day before, and if possible should be arranged so that the destination will be reached during the afternoon or evening. The journey, if not too long, will tire the players just enough to make them sleep well. It is not a good plan to make the trip two or three days before the game, as the excitement prevailing in the locality, and the change of surroundings and of food, are likely to have an injurious effect upon the players.

The team should be prepared with an outfit adaptable to any kind of weather conditions, special attention being given to the shoes and the cleats upon them. If the field is muddy or the weather rainy the suits should be light and the cleats upon the shoes long. If the weather is very cold it will be advantageous for the players to wear warm underwear.

Before tossing for the choice of goal or the kick-off the direction of the wind and the position of the sun should be noted, and also the tendency of the wind to increase or diminish late in the afternoon. In some localities the wind dies down as night approaches, and in this case the winner of the toss should choose the goal favored by the wind, whereas if the wind is likely to increase toward evening, the choice should be made so as to get the benefit of the wind in the last period.

When a team receives the kick-off with a favoring wind, or with the wind blowing across the field, good generalship on the part of the opposing team should cause it to place the kick-off to the side or corner of the field least favored, or to the windward side. If the kick is so placed the team receiving (provided the ball is run straight back from the point where it is caught) will be forced when it punts to kick the ball across the path of the wind to keep it from going out of bounds, while if the ball was kicked off to the other side, it could be returned by a punt diagonally across the field with the wind almost behind it. It is usually good generalship in any case for the kick-off to be placed to the side, because the man best able to run the ball back is usually placed directly in front of the goal, and it is wise to kick the ball where he cannot get it. It is also more difficult for the receiving team to get together and form interference at one side of the field than it is in the center, and the team kicking off can place its best tacklers, and an extra man or two, on the side toward which the kick-off is to be made.

In many respects a football game is very similar to a war, and good generalship is as important in one as it is in the other. Each scrimmage represents a battle in which the opposing forces are lined up opposite each other, one side defending itself against the attack of the other. The lines represent the infantry, and the backs can be likened to cavalry, moving quickly and able to charge the enemy at any spot or to rush to the support of any position attacked. The attacking quarterback or general should study well the defense of the enemy, and decide whether to force through their center, turn their flank by a quick movement, deceive them by feinting in one direction while the real attack is made at another spot, or transfer the battle to a more favorable locality by a punt. In making this decision he should take into consideration the condition of the field, the direction of the wind, and especially the position on the field with reference to the goal or side lines and the number of the down and the distance to be gained. If the wind is favorable and the ball is near the goal line which his team is defending, the battle should by all means be transferred to the enemy's territory by a punt, reserving ammunition and strength for an attack when an opportunity is gained within striking distance of the enemy's goal.

On fourth down, unless play is near the opponent's goal, the ball should be punted unless it is reasonably certain that the required distance for a first down can be gained. This should amount to almost absolute certainty when the team in possession of the ball is in its own territory.

If a team is able to hold the opponents and prevent their gaining, it is wise to punt often, especially if the team excels in a punting game; but when the opponents are the stronger and are able to make consistent gains by rushing the ball, the weaker team should retain the ball as long as possible whenever they gain possession of it. They should only punt when forced to do so on fourth down, because so long as the ball is kept away from their opponents the latter will be unable to make much headway or to score. Such tactics are also advisable when a team has a lead and is content to keep the other side from overtaking them, as it is very discouraging for a losing team, only a few points behind, to realize that the time is fast slipping away and that they may be unable to get a chance to use their plays to score before the whistle blows.

When rushing the ball, the quarter should choose one of the strongest plays for use on the first down—a play which is usually good for five or more yards—and generally such plays should be directed outside of tackle. If the defense of the opponents is scattered it may be advisable to send the first play through the line, but usually it is not wise to attempt to gain ten yards in four downs by bucking the line. If four or more yards are gained on the first trial, the remaining distance necessary for a first down can usually be secured by straight plays which can be depended on for steady and sure gains. If the play used on first down is unsuccessful an end run or a trick play should be used next; and if this is stopped without much gain a forward pass, a trick play, or a strong play outside tackle should be resorted to on the third down.

On fourth down, unless the quarter is practically certain of gaining the required distance, the ball should be punted unless it is near enough to the opponent's goal for a field-goal trial. A forward pass would be the proper play on fourth down near the opponent's goal when near the side of the field in such a position that a field goal would be difficult.

Good generalship on the part of the players, especially the captain, is as necessary when the team is on the defense as when rushing the ball. By studying the situation on every down, noting the distance to be gained and the part of the gridiron where the ball is situated, the defensive players can determine pretty closely what sort of tactics will be used in nearly every play. The backs particularly should be able to size up what play to look out for and can change their positions accordingly, closing in when expecting a line attack and moving back when a punt, a forward pass, or a trick play is likely to be pulled off. If the field and the ball are slippery, the defense should play in much closer than it would on a dry day, because end runs and fancy plays will be impossible under these conditions and the main strength of the attack will very likely consist of plays directed at the line.

All the defects in the team's play can be noted during the first half and corrected during the intermission, and the team which is in the hands of the best general, whether he be captain or coach, will usually show the greatest improvement as the game progresses.

The Kicking Game

While there are always quite a number of grandstand coaches attending almost every football game of any importance —people who later can tell their friends and the coaches of the teams just what mistakes were made and what ought to have been done at crucial stages of the game—there are comparatively few spectators who thoroughly understand sound football strategy. The percentage who really do know what it is all about is increasing wonderfully, but those who understand the game well are still in the minority, and even among the best and most experienced coaches there are differences of opinion on many points.

A great many coaches and critics believe in the kicking game. By this is meant that a team should always punt the ball in its own territory on first or second down, provided it has a good reliable punter. Their argument is that it is foolish for a team to try to rush the ball in its own territory, because they say it is a waste of energy, with small chance of being able to carry the ball to the other team's goal line without losing it. They argue that rushing the ball is more wearing and exhausting work than playing on the defense, and they further say that the opposing team learns the plays and how to stop them before the rushing team gets dangerously near to a touchdown. "Kick and wait for the breaks" is the motto of the advocates of the kicking game, and by breaks is usually meant a fumbled punt which the kicking team recovers. The kicking team does not like to rush the ball and expose its system of attack, or run the risk of losing the ball on a fumble, until by some lucky chance they secure the ball in the enemy's territory. Then they unloose their big guns, use their strongest plays, and try to score.

This strategy is all very good if a team has an excellent punter and a fast pair of ends to get down the field to prevent run-backs by the catcher of the punts. It is not good if a team is being outpunted, or if the kicks are being handled cleanly and rushed back by a clever safety man for good gains. The kicking game is also good when a team has the wind at its back, especially if the wind is fairly strong.

The arguments against the kicking game are that a team as a rule cannot score unless it has the ball, and the kicked ball is usually surrendered to the other team. It is further argued that there is no more chance that the catcher of punts will fumble than there is that he will run the ball back for a long gain or perhaps for a touchdown. Many good broken-field runners have done just that. Two teams may be very unevenly matched in weight and general ability, and yet if the weaker team has just as good a kicker as its opponents, plus a fleet pair of ends, a kicking game played by both teams would result in an even game, whereas if the stronger team rushed the ball until forced to punt it would no doubt run up a large score. It would seem that a stronger team is not making much headway by continually kicking instead of rushing. On the other hand the weaker team, while not able to make much headway by rushing, would probably be using poor judgment in punting on first and second down, because the stronger opponents cannot score while the weaker team retains possession of the ball and it would seem wise for the latter team to rush the ball for three downs before kicking even though little if any gain is made. It takes up time and keeps the ball out of the hands of the opponents, and is therefore good defensive strategy.

Opponents of the kicking game argue that a team might just as well rush the ball for at least two downs in its own territory because there is a chance on every play that the runner will get away for a long run, while in any case some gain is almost sure to be made, enabling the team at least to punt the ball from that much nearer the opponent's goal.

Moreover, many coaches and critics are of the opinion that defensive football is just as fatiguing as offensive play, and that a team by trying out its plays in its own territory, or at every opportunity, enables its field general to find out what plays in its repertoire work the best and what weaknesses there are in the opponent's defense, so that when he is within scoring distance of the opponent's goal he can take advantage of this knowledge.

Personally, I like to have my team rush the ball at every opportunity unless advantage can be taken of a strong wind or a nervous and butter-fingered safety man who is very likely to fumble. I believe that a team gets stronger and the plays work better the more the ball is rushed. The demoralizing effect on a defensive team of finding that they cannot stop their opponents and of seeing the lineman's stakes continually being moved closer to their goal is very great, whereas the rushing team gains confidence with every good gain or first down made. As an instance of this I will relate an experience I had while I was at Carlisle. The Indians were playing Dartmouth in the final game of the season. Dartmouth was undefeated and was disputing the Eastern championship with Harvard, which also had an unbroken record. Carlisle was supposed to be an easy mark for its opponents. In their own territory the Indians rushed the ball at every opportunity until forced to kick, and Dartmouth stopped their attack very well, scoring ten points to the Indians' seven in the first half. The Redskins, however, continued their rushing tactics in the second half, and gradually their offense became stronger and Dartmouth's defense weaker. The Indians found a couple of weak spots in the Dartmouth line, and they found that they had a couple of plays which Dartmouth could not stop. They carried the ball from where they received it on the kick-off—on three or four occasions nearly the length of the field—for touchdowns. In the latter part of the game they had their opponents completely demoralized and powerless to stop their plays, the final result being Carlisle 34, Dartmouth 10. It was the continual hammering of the Indians' attack which gradually battered down the defense, thus proving, to my mind, that it is foolish for a team to save its plays until some lucky break gives it the ball within striking distance of the opponent's goal.

Of course, when a team is rushing the ball in its own territory plays should not be used which require two or more players' handling the ball, and throwing forward passes which stand a chance of being intercepted should be avoided, unless they are extremely long ones equal to a punt. Only plays in which the possibility of fumbling is very small should be made use of there, and the best rule to follow is to play safe plays in your own territory, take more chances in the center of the field, and when near the opponent's goal use your best sure-gaining plays and make every play count.

GENERALSHIP

In closing I wish to impress upon all players, whether on the offense or defense, the importance of never letting down in their efforts.

> Do your darndest when you play,
>   Keep a-goin'.
> To take it easy doesn't pay,
>   Keep a-goin'.
> When the game is pretty tough,
> Don't you ever holler "nuff,"
> Show the world you have the stuff.
>   Keep a-goin'.
>
> If you strike a better bunch,
>   Keep a-goin'.
> You only need a harder punch,
>   Keep a-goin'.
> 'Tain't no use to stand and whine
> When they're coming through your line.
> Hitch your trousers up and climb,
>   Keep a-goin'.
>
> If the other team's on top,
>   Keep a-goin'.
> That's just the time you must not stop,
>   Keep a-goin'.
> 'S'pose they stop 'most every play:
> One good long run may win the day.
> To get discouraged doesn't pay,
>   Keep a-goin'.
>
> When it seems the game is lost,
>   Keep a-goin'.
> Do not stop at any cost—
>   Keep a-goin'.
> Don't ever think that you can't win it,
> A fightin' team is always in it.
> So don't let up a single minute,
>   Keep a-goin'!

Reprints of the Pop Warner Single-Wing Trilogy

A Course in Football for Players and Coaches: Offense
Reprints of the 1908 offense pamphlet, 1909 supplement & 1910 revision from Warner's groundbreaking correspondence course on the rudiments of football. Also includes Tom Benjey's interpretation of the birth and early evolution of the singlewing offense.
ISBN-10 0-9774486-5-7
ISBN-13 978-0-9774486-5-4

A Course in Football for Players and Coaches
Reprint of Warner's 1912 hardbound version of his correspondence course on the rudiments of football. Includes an early evolution of the single-wing offense.
ISBN-10 0-9774486-6-5
ISBN-13 978-0-9774486-6-1

Football for Coaches and Players
Reprint of Warner's 1927 hardbound classic on the rudiments of football. Includes evolved unbalanced-line single-wing and double-wing formations.
ISBN-10 0-9774486-4-9
ISBN-13 978-0-9774486-4-7

Watch for the release of Tom Benjey's upcoming exploration of the later lives of Carlisle Indian School stars. Who would become one of Eliot Ness's Untouchables? Which one would elope with a socialite?

Tuxedo Press
546 E Springville Rd
Carlisle, PA 17015
717-258-9733
www.LoneStarDietz.com

www.ingramcontent.com/pod-product-compliance
Lightning Source LLC
Chambersburg PA
CBHW031244290426
44109CB00012B/432